The Bullhearted Brand:
Building bullish restaurant brands that charge ahead of the herd

Joseph Szala

The Bullhearted Brand
Building Bullish Restaurant Brands That Charge Ahead of the Herd
A Szalapalooza, LLC Publication

Published by Szalapalooza, LLC
1387 Woodland Hills Drive
Atlanta, Georgia 30324
(717) 968-4846
www.szalapalooza.com

© 2021 Copyright by Joseph Szala and Szalapalooza, LLC.
Printed in the United States of America.

First Edition May 2021

All rights reserved. No part of this book may be reproduced or transmitted in any form or by any means electronic or mechanical including photocopying, recording, or by an information storage or retrieval system, without the written permission of the publisher except where permitted by law.

ISBN 978-0-9906155-3-8

Library of Congress Control Number: 2021918115

Layout and design by Joseph Szala
Cover art and illustrations by Joseph Szala
Edited by Cathy McMahen
Indexing by Julia Torres
This book is typeset in Garamond Premier Pro, Proxima Nova, and Oswald type families.

To my wonderful wife who inspires me daily and encourages me to be better. And to Elsa for keeping my lap, and heart, warm.

Contents

(Very) Foreword............13

What's with the Bulls?...............17

What This Book Is, and What It Isn't................17

Bull Story: Jallikattu..................19

1. The 7 Branding Truths...................21

Bull Story: Bull in a China Shop...................22

Truth Be Told..................24

01 / Your definition of "branding" is wrong...........24

02 / Good food & good service is not unique........27

03 / Table stakes are not differentiators.............28

04 / People make brands, companies only guide them .. 30

05 / You may not need "branding" 32

06 / Humans love human brands 34

07 / Branding influences everything................. 35

2. The Golden Lasso 38

Bull Story: Three Bulls and the Lion 39

Unity is the Gold Standard 41

The Golden Lasso: Creating Unbreakable Bonds between Patrons and Brands........................ 42

Getting Started with the Right Mindset.............. 46

3. People Power Brands 49

Bull Story: 95-96 Chicago Bulls..................... 50

Branding Is not Just a Marketing Focus 53

Good Leader, Bad Leader......................... 54

Who Will Champion This Brand? 56

Who Are Your Brand's Stakeholders?............... 58

Patron: Identifying and Understanding Your Best Friends 59

The Multiple Layers of Patrons...................... 61

The Patron Most Brands Forget.................... 64

In Real Life: How a Sustainable Brand Fails to Sustain its People 66

4. Positioning for Success 69

Bull Story: Javanese Bull. 70

Why Positioning Still Matters 72

Competition Is a Good Thing; Learn to Love It 75

Your Competition Isn't What You May Think 77

Analyze Your Competition with Honesty and Clarity . . 80

The Perceptual Map and How to Find Your Whitespace. . 83

Effective Positioning Should Fuel Innovation 86

In Real Life: How Hubris Killed a Pizza Brand Primed to Rise Up. 88

What's Next?. 90

5. Core Layers of a Brand. 91

Bull Story: Ferdinand 92

The Layers of a Bullhearted Brand 94

Purpose: Why Your Brand Exists and Why It Matters . . 96

Finding Your Purpose: Archetypes 99

Finding Your Purpose: Five Whys 104

Personality: The Unique Attitude That Sets You Apart 107

How to Identify Your Brand's Personality Traits. 111

Gandhi and Che: Wildly Different, Oddly Similar. 114

Product: What the Brand Brings to the World 116

In Real Life: How a Brand Misalignment Created a not so

Yummy QSR Failure 123

6. Presentation. 127

Bull Story: Sacred Cows 128

Presenting The Presentation Layer. 131

Everything Matters. Every. Single. Thing. Matters. 133

Naming is Hard and That's Okay. 136

What Makes for a Great Name?. 139

Four Examples of Fantastic Restaurant Brand Names 144

Beyond the Logo: Think Visual Language 147

Four Hallmarks of a Strong Visual Identity. 150

Menu Design: What's on the Menu?. 156

Menu Design: What's the Menu On?. 159

Location, Location, Location. 162

Four Walls, Limitless Opportunities. 165

Digital Is as Important as Physical. 167

The Fifth Wall: Augmented and Virtual Reality 171

Activating the Brand with Internal Stakeholders. 175

In Real Life: Simmering Down an Authentic Flavor of Sai Gon. 177

Recap & What's Next. 180

7. Propelling Brands Ahead of the Herd. 182

Bull Story: Parade of Toritos 183

The Thing about Marketing 185

There Is no Magic Bullet. 188

The Marketing Ecosystem in Action 192

Understanding the Patron Journey. 195

Evergreen and Campaign Marketing 200

The 3 Components of Remarkable Creative 202

Social Media Isn't Advertising .206

Cheap Marketing Isn't Cheap. 210

Discounts Discount the Brand 212

In Real Life: A Promotion Without Purpose is Nothing to Celebrate. 215

8. Evolving Brands. 218

Bull Story: The Clever Bull 219

The Difference between Rebranding and Brand Evolution 222

Identifying the Gaps between Current State and Desired State. 225

The Hardest Thing to Do: Remove Excess. 227

Changing with the Changing Times 230

Activate and Celebrate Internally and Externally 234

What Does the Future Hold? 237

In Real Life: Evolving a Classic QSR with Easygoing Vibes 241

9. Charging Ahead. 252

Bull Story: Babe the Blue Ox 253

Finding the Right Partners 254

Onboard partners for success 259

Final Thoughts 262

Further Reading & Listening 264

Index 269

The Bullhearted Brand:
Building Bullish Restaurant Brands That Charge Ahead of the Herd

(Very) Foreword

In 2010, I moved from Pennsylvania to Atlanta, Georgia. It was in the wake of the Great Recession, and I had resolved to make some significant changes in my life. The move was the biggest of those changes. While on the eleven hour drive with my life in tow, I had time to thoroughly evaluate just about every aspect of my life from personal to professional. It was during this time that I solidified the next steps I'd take once I arrived at my new home.

That uninterrupted time allowed me to fully consider the future of Vigor, the agency I had built for seven years and recently watched crumble from an eight person design studio to a one-man show. In my humbled yet optimistic state, I made some clear resolutions for what was next for Vigor. They all boiled down to one general philosophy: practice what I preach.

Vigor's business model had been basic. We designed brand identities, collateral, and websites for companies who needed those things. From wedding retailers to pharmaceutical powerhouses, we took anyone and everyone who would write a check. Not a bad idea in theory, but it posed some pretty big issues. The fact is, we stood for nothing, and we weren't able to foster expertise in any one direction. What's worse is, this approach was antithetical to what we advised our clients. We weren't practicing what we preached. That needed to change immediately.

Upon my arrival in Atlanta, I began to redirect the foundations of Vigor and its future. I took myself through the same branding process I used with my clients. This netted out a very clear path for the agency and a passion-driven niche. My love for what restaurants bring to this world would be combined with my adoration of branding and marketing. Vigor would become laser-focused on providing best-in-class branding and marketing for the restaurant world.

With the newfound vigor for Vigor and a clear focus, I began recrafting every touchpoint. I then got to work on adapting the company's process, beliefs, and thought-leadership articles for the restaurant industry. Before I knew it, I was writing a book.

Fire It Up: Building Restaurant Brands That Blaze was a small, but mighty, guide to creating restaurant brands. Its content was fueled by a mix of frustration and idealism. After all, I did just watch my agency fall apart. I wasn't exactly the most positively charged person. With *Fire It Up*, I sought to clear up prevalent misunderstandings with what branding is and what it can do, while equipping our clients with a foundation to engage in a successful branding process. Secondly I wanted to wave the flag of expertise and a focused niche for the agency. It worked.

It's over 10 years later and while many things have changed, my love for restaurants and Vigor's expertise have only increased. I'm less frustrated and much more idealistic. My passion for building successful, distinctive restaurant brands has grown in size and strength with the momentum of a charging bull.

It's that passion that led me to reevaluate *Fire It Up* from tone of voice through content. *Fire It Up* didn't deliver on Vigor's personality and passion enough to be a valuable resource for readers and the agency. Combined with new ideas in branding and marketing, a lot more experience, and massive shifts in the consumer landscape, the book was borderline irrelevant. I made up my mind to rewrite it with renewed vigor.

In 2018, when I approached a rewrite, I ended up on another path. I found myself deep in a rabbit hole that sparked an idea for a different book. One that used fables and folklore from across cultures that used bulls as characters to deliver lessons. I curated and wrote a small book of stories based on these fables and folklore tales, and from those stories, I gleaned brand truths that should be used in building cultures inside of restaurant organizations. That book was also a representation of our hearts and our passions and served as an introduction to working with Vigor. I titled it, *Running with the Bulls*.

Fire It Up no longer makes sense for the name of this book for a number of reasons. Since 2010, Vigor has come into its own with courageous, principled, and empathetic values. These values define what Vigor means to us, to our clients, and, I hope, anyone who encounters the brand. With those values, our name, and a clearly defined vision, we found a totem that embodied every part of Vigor: a bull. That spirit animal serves as many things for this agency, and it also serves as the basis for the book's new title: *The Bullhearted Brand - Building Bullish Brands That Charge Ahead of the Herd*.

What's with the Bulls?

Bulls are found around the world. They do everything from plowing fields to grow food to being worshipped. They serve as metaphors and representatives of traits good and bad. It's safe to say that everyone has heard a story or a phrase that involves a bull. Bulls are recognizable and prevalent.

There are many traits attributed to bulls from being passionate and unyielding to fertile and unstoppable. Bulls make their way into many fables and parables as a result of their numerous traits and ubiquity. Additionally, the bull represents financial markets that are thriving. This makes the bull a perfect mechanism to deliver brand thinking that results in success. I will also point out that the bull is Vigor's spirit animal and the subject matter of our agency's brand identity.

Throughout this book, I intermingle the fables and folklore I used for *Running with the Bulls* book, with expertise and guidance on how to build bullish brands. In addition to those bull stories, are a few more that I curated to help flesh out a fuller suite of bull-inspired knowledge. These bull stories serve to reinforce the knowledge and thinking that will help you dig deep into the driving passions and purpose that will serve as the epicenter of your brand.

What This Book Is, and What It Isn't

The restaurant industry is a constantly evolving one with trends that come and go quicker than froyo melts. At the same time, consumer behaviors continue to shift from year to year, driven by new technology and cultural influences. It wasn't even ten years ago that Instagram launched, and now it's one of the most influential marketing channels today (as of the time of this writing.) As it reaches a pinnacle, we know that there is most likely a contender waiting to be the next one up. It can be maddening to try to keep up, but that's the reality of our world.

No matter what technologies come and go, and no matter where consumer's interests are focused, strong brands will brave the day. Now, more than ever, creating strong restaurant brands is critical to success. Whether you're launching the vision you've been working on for years, or you're solidifying the foundations of an existing concept, a strong brand is good business. A restaurant brand built with the information in this book is brilliant business.

The Bullhearted Brand is a guide to developing your restaurant's brand from concept through growth. My goal in writing it is to equip you with the guiding principles, thinking, and honesty to craft your own successful restaurant brand, or to thoroughly understand the components and theories to successfully guide the process with a trusted partner.

Through data, experience, and examples, I'll show you how to create a remarkable, successful restaurant experience and brand. Whether you're endeavoring to do it yourself (highly ill-advised) or working with an agency, *The Bullhearted Brand* will give you the means to maximize your brand's potential.

This book is not a play-by-play workbook meant to systematize creating a restaurant brand. Successful brands are built from the heart, and that's not a component that can be emulated or faked. Branding takes time, effort, and honesty to do right. While I can give you the components and framework, this book cannot provide all the details and nuances it requires to develop your restaurant's brand from beginning to end. Trusted, experienced partners are the key to success. At the end of this book, I've listed some agencies and studios we know to be fantastic partners. Oh, and my company, Vigor, is a damn good option, too.

Bull Story: Jallikattu

The Story

Jallikattu is a traditional event practiced in the Indian state of Tamil Nadu as part of the Pongal celebrations for Mattu Pongal day. The event involves releasing a bull (Bos indicus), such as one of the Pulikulam or Kangayam breeds, into a crowd of people. Multiple participants attempt to grab the large hump on the bull's back with both arms and hang on while the bull bucks and thrashes, trying to escape their grasp. Participants hold the hump for as long as possible, attempting to bring the bull to a stop. In some cases, participants must ride long enough to remove flags that have been affixed to the bull's horns.

Jallikattu is a test of strength, endurance, and bravery. There is much competition to engage with the bull and stop it, but many fail. Throughout the event's history have been incidents of injury and even death in both the participants and animals. As a result, animal rights organizations did call for a ban, which was granted by courts several times. However, people protested against the ban, and a new ordinance was made in 2017 to allow a continuation of the sport.[1]

---

[1] "Jallikattu," Wikipedia, last revised January 15, 2021, https://en.wikipedia.org/w/index.php?title=-Jallikattu&oldid=1000586284.

The Lesson: Have the Courage to Grab the Bull by the Horns

Nothing in this world is easy and creating a brand from scratch, or evolving an existing one, is no different. Too often, people see brand development as a visual undertaking and completely overlook or ignore all the groundwork that must be laid in order to endeavor successfully. Whether it's out of a desire for speed or an honest lack of understanding, matters not. Branding isn't as easy as making something look pretty—a fact I'll unravel as we get into this book.

Much like the Jallikattu, branding is about wrangling ideas and people into submission. Not submission in the exact sense of this sport, rather submitting to an aligned vision and strategy. Only when a strategy is set and the team aligned, can one design a visual presentation that will connect. But what does it take to wrestle that strategy into clarity?

It takes guts to be different— to zig when everyone else wants to zag. It takes principled leadership to guide the team and foster belief and buy-in. And it takes empathy to find common ground and devise ways of communicating core values to people in their language.

I encourage you to conjure up your inner Pongal celebrant and dare to grab the bull by the hump. Wrangle in the ideas, passion, and various ideas and formulate the foundations of building a bullish brand. Lead your team with principled confidence, and empower them to let go of their personal notions so they may adopt the foundations of the brand.

It takes a bullhearted person to build bullish brands.

1. The 7 Branding Truths

Bull Story: Bull in a China Shop

The Story

We've all heard the phrase, "like a bull in a china shop." The bull, being large and without grace, finds himself in a place full of breakables. Tragedy ensues. The phrase is used to describe someone who's reckless and clumsy, crashing through something with no regard for the destruction caused.

The first known use of the phrase "a bull in a china shop" is in the novel *Jacob Faithful* written by Frederick Marryat in 1834.[2] It's believed that the phrase originated from actual real-life scenarios. In the 17th century, cattle were often brought into the market area of London.[3] Sometimes they would get loose and stray into shops that sold delicate goods, like fine china. They would wreak havoc on the shop's wares.

Even though this once common phrase isn't used as much today, it

---

[2] Rajiv Bhalla, "What's the Origin of the Phrase 'A Bull in a China Shop'?" Times of India, October 14, 2006, https://www.google.com/search?q=heb&oq=heb&aqs=chrome..69i57j0l7.10835j1j4&sourceid=chrome&ie=UTF-8.

[3] Ibid.

still perfectly embodies the idea of someone dealing with a delicate problem in an overly aggressive, and possibly clumsy, manner. To this day it's still considered a negative description, but we think there's another angle.

The Lesson: Don't Be Afraid to Break the Rules

Being described as "a bull in a china shop" isn't something that would make one happy. When taken at face value, a bull in a china shop is a bad thing. But we like to think of it in a different way. We think it's a positive and the root of remarkable ideas.

Like a lot of other industries, the restaurant space has a multitude of perceived immutable truths: showing a fork in a logo, menus touting "local" and "craft," the need for a dining area in the restaurant space. These are supposed rules to live by, but why? Because they worked before, so they must work again? Because everyone else is doing it, so it must work? Whatever the answer may be, the majority of restaurateurs never question these rules and take them as the law of the land.

The plates of china in this metaphor represent these so-called rules, and they're barriers to innovation and new thinking. For a restaurant to thrive and succeed, it must bring something to market that's new and remarkable. But that's impossible if you're following the rules. Those rules beget more of the same which results in plateaus at best, failure at worst. The only way to break the mold is to destroy the status quo by challenging those rules.

So we say, be a bull in a china shop, and break those plates because if you spend all your time trying to fit in, you'll spend all of your money trying to stand out. And when you destroy that china shop, it's going to make some noise that people can't ignore.

Truth Be Told

Throughout my 17+ years at the helm of Vigor, time and again I encounter thinking and practices that hold leaders back from crafting successful brand experiences. They either hinder progress significantly or prevent it entirely. I spend a lot of time coaching our clients out of that thinking and those practices to guide them into the right mindset for crafting their brands to charge ahead.

In this section, I list seven brand truths that you need to understand in order to create successful brand experiences. Under each truth, I've supplied the details and knowledge for you to absorb and understand so you can charge forward with the right thinking.

Yes, the irony of starting this chapter of truths, or rules, off with a bull story that challenges you to break the rules is not lost on me. Believe it or not, it's on purpose. The only way you can break the rules is if you fully understand them. Just as the character Howard Roark, Ayn Rand's famous protagonist in *The Fountainhead*, developed a deep understanding of construction before becoming a heroic architect, you must learn the fundamentals of strong brands before you can break the china.

01 / Your definition of "branding" is wrong

Don't worry, the dictionary has it wrong, too, and so do many companies who label themselves "branding agencies." I'm not being nitpicky or splitting hairs just to display depth of knowledge or prey on a technicality. I push the issue because misunderstanding the true definition of "branding" creates a scenario of buyer's remorse at best and outright failure at worst. Either way, you're left unhappy and with less money in the bank. I don't want that, and I'm certain neither do you.

The proliferation of "branding" as an integral component to business success simultaneously elevated the power of design for business and created a gap of misunderstanding and miscommunication between agencies and their clients. You must know exactly what you're buying before making the leap into hiring an agency partner and spending the necessary time successful branding requires. A lot of agencies sell the buzzword of "branding," but in reality, they only offer graphic design services. I'm not saying the tactic is malicious or intentionally misleading, but that doesn't excuse the reality, and it certainly doesn't absolve selling half-baked services.

Yes, graphic design is a part of the bigger branding picture, but it's only one of many facets that comprise a fully-formed brand. The outputs from graphic design are the things people can see—the "pretty pictures" as some call them. It's the logo, menus, website, and other visual communications that represent the restaurant in the world. They're what grabs attention and attracts people to the restaurant. It's easy to see how those elements became mislabeled as "branding." Their tangibility and visual appeal make it seem they are branding. They are not.

The visual outputs we all see from a restaurant cumulatively fall under the term "brand identity." It's the perfect label if you think about it. This is the visual identity of a brand, just like me wearing a black v-neck t-shirt and slim-fit jeans creates my look to the world around me, logos and supporting graphic elements create a restaurant's look to their audience.

Brand identity is a critical component of the branding discipline. If the visual communications don't properly communicate the various aspects of the restaurant, that brand fails to attract and connect with people. But to ensure an identity communicates effectively, one must possess an understanding of what should be communicated. And that's the core of what "branding" truly entails.

Every business creates a brand simply by existing. A brand is an amalgamation of what a company does, how they do it, and, the most important element for today's audiences, why the company exists. Most businesses ace the first two components of what they do and how they do it. Rare is the brand that identifies why they exist and why it matters. Therefore, "branding" is the process of excavating a company's purpose, then aligning their products, services, people, personality, and communications to bolster and build that purpose in the world.

"Purpose" is one of the toughest components to identify and excavate. I think it's because most companies' sole purpose is to make money and food with little else. While the potential of financial gain is an obvious goal for existence, that thinking myopically focuses everything on good food and good service, and nothing more. Cue the hero shots of sizzling steaks and the penchant for following trends like Blank and Blank restaurant names (more on that later.)

Today's restaurant landscape is fiercely competitive. That reality, combined with the subjectivity and fickleness of flavor trends and service, aren't enough to build a restaurant brand primed for growth. At some point, someone will think your food is garbage, and the service won't always meet their needs at that moment, at that time. In one fell swoop, good food and good service are erased, and if nothing else exists to position your restaurant, your restaurant brand fails. When done successfully, restaurant brands build something stronger and deeper than good food and good service.

02 / Good food & good service is not unique

When the world was smaller and a town's center was the core of commerce, competition wasn't a big worry. There existed one or two businesses to supply each need, and maybe one or two competitors. You got your meat from the butcher, your bread from the baker, and your other sundries from the general store. It was pretty simple. At that time, an enterprising go-getter simply had to paint a name on a sign, and tack it to the façade of a building. More often than not, it was an existing business handed down through the family. Doors opened, customers came in, and you had a successful enterprise.

That era is long gone and with it the simplicity of only needing to tout basic features.

In today's world, competition is more than a potential threat. It's a fierce reality. And it's not one or two competitors that restaurants face. It's a heavy mix of new, local concepts, longstanding staples, and both regional and national chains. There's a pizza shop on every corner and Starbucks down the street. You can go down the list of food categories and put multiple ticks next to each one. Hell, consumers are technically competitors because they can cook for themselves at home and cut out the middleman. Even the most innovative, life-changing inventions and companies quickly have competition nipping at their heels. Put bluntly, whatever it is you want to bring to market, it's already been done numerous times. An idea based on food alone isn't unique.

That's not to say there isn't room for innovation in the restaurant space. There is always room for something new, and there are always areas to be improved if you're keeping your eyes open and ears to the ground. What I am saying is that the world isn't begging for another pizza shop or Chinese restaurant. Therefore, your restaurant isn't filling a gap in product availability, and it's not going to fill the need for stellar service. Good product and good service are expectations, not selling points.

I know what you're thinking, "but Joseph, you haven't tried MY pizza. It's the best, and you're going to love it!" I'd respond the same way I do every time I'm confronted with this statement, "I'm sure you think it is. I bet you think your kids aren't ugly either." A bit inflammatory, but that's on purpose. (I'm sure your kids are beautiful.) The reason for the jolting response is this: for your pizza to be "the best", the pizza I love and buy all the time is not "the best." In short, you're telling me I'm wrong. Do me a favor, go tell your partner they are wrong and see how that goes.

Now take that tactic and multiply it across a large group of people. This is the essence of how the majority of restaurant brands position and market themselves to the public. This is why most marketing efforts are fruitless and why a large percentage of restaurants fail. This approach is rooted in telling people they are wrong.

What makes a brand unique is its reason for being, the passion that it believes in and lives daily. Honesty and trustworthiness are what attract consumers of today, and it's what sets you apart from the competition. Your brand's purpose is what makes it unique, not the food, not the service.

03 / Table stakes are not differentiators

Too often we're confronted with a trend-following vision for a new concept. Farm to table, chef-driven, craft burgers…the list is seemingly never-ending and always changing. The thinking makes a lot of sense: capitalize on what's buzzing with consumers at that moment. Build a concept quickly and scale it as fast as possible. However, trends come and go, and with them the concepts that didn't have the foundations behind exploiting the consumer's fickle attention.

Trends fluctuate, but consumer expectations are much less transient. Expectations are in constant growth influenced by trends, culture, and other factors. Yes, trends can and do affect consumer expectations, but they are soon absorbed into expectations. And consumer expectations are not differentiators, they're table stakes.

In gambling, a "table stake" is the cost of being at the table. It's the bottom line requirement to play the game. As trends take hold and proliferate, they morph from a unique feature that gets attention into an expectation; a table stake. When a trend becomes an expectation, concepts built upon that trend lose their luster and their market share. While there may be wild successes in the immediate future, the long term is bleak if the brand doesn't have anything deeper than the exploiting trend.

You can take almost every trend and find the shortcomings of a brand that led it. Better burgers, chef-driven fast casuals, frozen yogurt, and farm-to-table concepts all had a lot of momentum at one time, but each category is currently in the denouement of its trend. What's left are the concepts that told a better, deeper story, and the remnants of the ones that didn't.

In the last year alone, the United States has seen the rise of many trends. The larger ones make their way into expectations, the smaller ones simply fade out (e.g. frozen yogurt, poke bowls.) One of the larger trends in recent history was the craft food movement and the rise of chef-driven cuisine at fast-casual restaurants. These "features" are no longer unique as most concepts tout the very same things. Even "farm to table" has been watered down and muddied with questionable practices that leave consumers questioning the validity of the claims. In today's reality, simply making claims like these isn't enough. Consumers need to know the details. They need to know how, and, most importantly, why the brand has chosen to be chef-driven or farm-to-table. How does it align with the restaurant's values? Why does it matter to the restaurant, and why should it matter to the person?

Through abuse and over-use, we, as an industry, have neutered the believability and power of words like "craft" and "farm-to-table." Brands that built their restaurant on those foundations alone now feel the pain of frustration as competitors nip at their heels or successfully strip market share away from them. And there's not much that can be done because trends aren't differentiators.

There will always be an influx of trends in food categories and methodologies. What won't change is the consumer's demand for honesty and a clear show of values from a brand. Restaurants that adopt this thinking and build their brands on honest values will continue to thrive. Brands are deeper than the product they sell and the manner in which they sell it.

04 / People make brands, companies only guide them

Many branding conversations focus on the company, from product through service. Little is spoken about the people that we try to attract with branding. Branding and marketing go much deeper than trying to figure out what makes people tick and how to "trick" them into buying. By understanding what brands truly bring to people's lives, you can build one that does way more than satiate hunger.

Today, people have a constant stream of information and messages pounding them every second. Concurrently, they have become curators of their own life stories, projecting the persona they want people to see. Think about Instagram or Facebook and the images shared, conversations had, and connections made. The reality is that the life you see on these platforms is a highlight reel. It's a purposefully curated picture of a life devoid of any negatives or elements the person doesn't wish for you to see.

As curators, people adopt the brands that align with their values as a means to portray another nuance to their personality and projected self. They seek out brands that will add traits or nuances to their persona so the world sees them how they wish. This may seem farfetched or a bit of a stretch until you really think about the choices you make and the reason behind those decisions. For instance, why buy the BMW when a Kia is a perfectly fine automobile? They both get you from point A to point B with similar amenities and features. One buys a BMW because it says that they appreciate the finer things, design, and engineering, and have realized enough success to afford the luxury. Everyone makes choices based on what that brand will project to the world about who they want to think they are. Restaurant brands are no different.

When a restaurant brand is created with a purpose, it exudes personality traits and attitude. These traits are exactly what people look for when shifting towards advocacy. Think of Starbucks or Chipotle. The commonality between these two brands is the strength of the personalities they put into the world. It's not the quality of the product. A Chipotle advocate enjoys the food, but also the story of sustainability which helps her feel like she's doing her part while displaying to the world a notion of a "concerned world citizen." Starbucks exudes the attitude of a go-getter who's picky and demands customizability.

This reality should immediately shift your thinking of what we do when we craft a brand. Without a deep understanding of a core group of people you wish to attract, branding is an exercise in art, and art alone. While art is fantastic, and I do love it, it's not a sound business strategy. Focusing on people, their projected selves, and their perceptions of your brand will give unique insights on how to lasso them closer to the brand with messaging, marketing, and every other part of the business.

It's not the food you sell or the service you provide. It's very much the reason you do it in the first place and how you support that reason with actions, choices, and business practices. It should also spark the question as to whether or not you need an intense, deep branding process.

05 / You may not need "branding"

Is engaging in a formal branding process necessary for your situation? The answer could very well be, "no, no it's not." You may only need an identity designed for your restaurant—the aforementioned "painted name on a sign, tacked to a wall." The right path for your restaurant involves an understanding of the purpose of branding as a whole.

Branding is best suited for restaurants that are looking to grow. Whether that's multi-unit or franchise, branding creates a strategic, unified experience across a network of restaurant locations. That's not meant to insinuate that each location is a mirror image or machine-stamped replica of a design. The days where that is appealing are in the past. However, the brand experiences must be tied together in multiple ways to affect and grow the overarching brand giving consumers a way to categorize it in their mind.

For restaurant groups that have multiple concepts under an umbrella, branding still has vital benefits. The structure of this scenario is a bit different though. Each restaurant must be allowed to have its own brand experience while the umbrella company holds the threads that make said restaurant part of the family. In this situation, the restaurant group must be known for the types of experiences it produces, and the type of service it delivers. This is still branding, even though each individual restaurant carries its own identity.

A single-unit restaurant is a different beast. Realizing a return on the investment in this scenario is difficult based on volume and numbers alone. There is only so much business that can be done at one location that quickly causes a plateau. Restaurants like these are usually mom-and-pop concepts that are family-run. In these instances, an identity design can do well.

An identity, or brand identity/visual identity, comprises a logo, color palette, typography, and various other elements to comprise a visual look and feel. These can be designed without a brand strategy. Instead, a designer relies on the information passed from the client to create a creative brief, or outline, of the restaurant's details. From this foundation, the designer can create some great looks for the restaurant that elevate it past other mom-and-pops in the local market. A strong identity design and an understanding of good business practices can result in a sustainable restaurant business. The key word is "sustainable," meaning it won't necessarily grow, but it shouldn't fail so long as it's maintained.

Chances are that sustenance isn't the goal. Most enterprising restaurateurs want much more than a single unit. Since you're reading this book, you more than likely want to create something that you can build and grow beyond that moment. If that sounds anything like what you're dreaming, then engaging in a detailed branding process is an absolute requirement. Good thing you're reading this book.

06 / Humans love human brands

What we're really attempting to do when developing brands is strengthen connectivity to consumers. If you boil it down, that's what it's all about. Brands that connect with people are brands that succeed in growing strong. The best way to connect with a person is to be empathetic, interesting, and align with similar values. But how can a company, a non-human entity, relate on these levels?

If you stop to think about it, brands actually do display features similar to a human. They have a personality and a passion: looks, feelings, offerings, and more. They perform actions, engage with the world around them, and they age. Humans, and brands, seek out like-minded people to befriend, associate with, and love. It only makes sense that a human serves as the best metaphor when discussing and creating brands.

We, as humans, have values. We are drawn to others that have those values. From the circumstantial like where one is born or lived to deeper level associations like politics and religion, we are a tribal species that require interaction with others to thrive. In the later part of the twentieth century, and into the twenty-first, humans have been attracted to brands for seemingly surface-level reasons. When you dig deeper into the psychology of the matter, it becomes clear that it's actually the human traits of a brand that attract people, and not their products and services.

Using a "human" as a lens through which to guide branding a restaurant gives a unique and powerful perspective. The metaphor adds the necessary weight and intricacies in creating a truly successful restaurant brand. It's an essential tool to focus your thinking and empower you to set a foundation for success.

Throughout the *Bullhearted Brand*, we'll use human-related terminology to develop the key platforms that comprise a multi-faceted restaurant brand. If I'm being completely honest, we'll also use bovine-related terminology, too. The bull serves as the brand mark for Vigor, and I can't resist a good pun. So, please, bear with me...or bull with me.

07 / Branding influences everything

If you haven't gathered already, there are numerous moments to miss the mark when it comes to developing a restaurant brand. Yet, I've seen many amazing restaurant brands in my time. They're found across the world in cities big and small. Successful restaurant brands are the ones that use brand strategy to influence every part of the company. And may very well be the most important nuance to remember when it comes to developing your own restaurant brand.

Building a strong brand strategy takes time and honesty with oneself, that you will soon learn. But, as they say, the best-laid plans of mice and men often go awry. No adage could be truer with regard to branding a restaurant. As I stated in earlier truths, a brand is something that's molded by every element of the restaurant's experience. Those elements create perceptions in the consumer's mind and drive the formation of stronger bonds through shared values. In weak or failed restaurant experiences, the root of the weakness is usually found deeper within the experience (e.g. poor operations, boring product mix, etc.)

How does the menu reflect the personality and purpose established in the strategy? How do the interiors create visual, tactile, and aural ties to the brand's identity and personality? When a guest is created, how does that reflect the unique personality of the brand? These questions, and many more, need to be asked once the brand strategy is established. Yet, more often than not, they aren't. And that is where most branding efforts miss the mark.

All partners involved in the restaurant should be aligned on the foundations of the brand. They must fire on the same cylinders instead of dividing off into their camps. This requires strong leadership that believes and buys into the brand and what it means to build a brand over time and across disciplines. When leaders understand that branding influences every part of the business, amazing concepts are realized. They grow quickly and they amass loyal followers. Divided concepts may hit a stride for a small amount of time, but they inevitably fall apart.

Going through the branding process, then onboarding every partner ensures a collective momentum towards success. With a clear foundation and understanding of how the strategy affects every facet of the business, restaurant companies can guide the present and future effectively. That has numerous measurable results from optimizing budget investment through building equity in the event of an acquisition. That's just the surface.

An investment in brand strategy from the top-down and bottom-up is the key to success in any industry. In the restaurant space, it separates the winners from the losers.

2. The Golden Lasso

Bull Story: Three Bulls and the Lion

The Story

There is an Aesop's fable about three bulls and a lion. For an unknown amount of time, a hungry lion had been intently watching three bullocks feeding in an open field. Even though their sharp horns, tough hooves, and greater number gave him little hope of eating them, the possibility of a good meal kept him nearby waiting for the opportunity. Every time he tried to attack, their strength in numbers always proved too great. He'd retreat defeated and embarrassed. The bullocks remained safe and sound.

Then one day, the bullocks had an argument. They bickered and quarreled until they stomped away, each one convinced they didn't need the other two. The hungry lion came back to check in on the group and licked his chops from afar, but instead of a well-fortified group, he found them in separate corners of the field. They were as far from one another as they could get.

One by one, the lion seized the opportunity to attack. This time, success and a good meal were his for the taking. The bullocks had eliminated their collective strength making their demise inevitable.

The Lesson: United You Thrive, Divided You Dive

You can't beat a unified front. When all parties in an organization work together with a clear purpose and reason for being, that brand is primed to fight the competition and win. If division creeps in, the brand weakens and has little chance to grow and fend off stronger brands.

Division can come in many forms. It can be the new employee who likes the company but has their own ideas on how to do things better. Rather than following protocol and due process, the employee jumps in feet first and starts to tinker. Even if there are times where the outcome sparks positive change, the very nature of this approach creates division. No good.

Another way division can happen is when a brand's leadership is misaligned on critical initiatives and goals. This is usually the case when all strategic platforms aren't clearly defined. There may be a common understanding of what kind of food is served and the method in which it's served. Maybe there's even a strong understanding of what makes the brand well-positioned in the market. But those are only two components of a bigger brand picture. Not having a clear understanding of every facet of the brand leaves the door open for disagreement and division. Can you hear the lion coming?

There's no shortage of brands who establish what they do and how to do it. Good product with good service is the baseline for any decent business. That's not enough, though. Establish why you exist and instill that belief throughout the organization. Create believers in your brand within the company's ranks, and develop strong unity throughout. Then, when the predators come to feast, your "herd" will have no problem defeating them.

Unity is the Gold Standard

At startup, most companies are relatively easy to create and steer. The restaurateur's vision is easily communicated and stakeholders are fully engaged. However, as the restaurant marches towards opening, the size of stakeholders and responsibilities begins to steamroll. If not managed properly, the beginnings of the brand go from a singular vision shared by all, to a chaotic, disjointed smattering of ideas. This creates a brand built on shaky ground.

The only way to craft and build strong restaurant brands is through a constant focus on establishing and developing unity inside and outside the organization. To craft a united brand requires a focus on authentic feelings and information, a pinch of creativity, and the courage to make some tough choices. These traits are even more critical when discussing a brand that has history and years of equity built.

Branding is a top-down endeavor, meaning that it starts with the leader of the organization, then infiltrates every part of the organization, adding nuance and strength along the way. From the very moment a new restaurant is conceived, a brand begins to form. That means the process and effort of developing a united brand start immediately.

Brand unity is realized when all stakeholders, internal and external, have a complete understanding of the brand and share its passion deeply. It's not solely a visual endeavor. All aspects of the restaurant must work in unison to create and guide the perceptions of what said brand stands for and why it matters. That means operations, marketing, and leadership must be marching under the same flag, to the same beat. But what beat, and how do you identify it?

Throughout this section, we'll take you through the mechanics of a united brand and how one is built element by element.

The Golden Lasso: Creating Unbreakable Bonds between Patrons and Brands

Many experts have attempted to visualize what brand infrastructure looks like. I've seen pyramids with stacked components, stacked arrows, flowcharts, and yes, even the beloved Venn diagram. Hey, we're actually guilty as well. That is until we put the focus and energy on developing a diagram that would effectively communicate

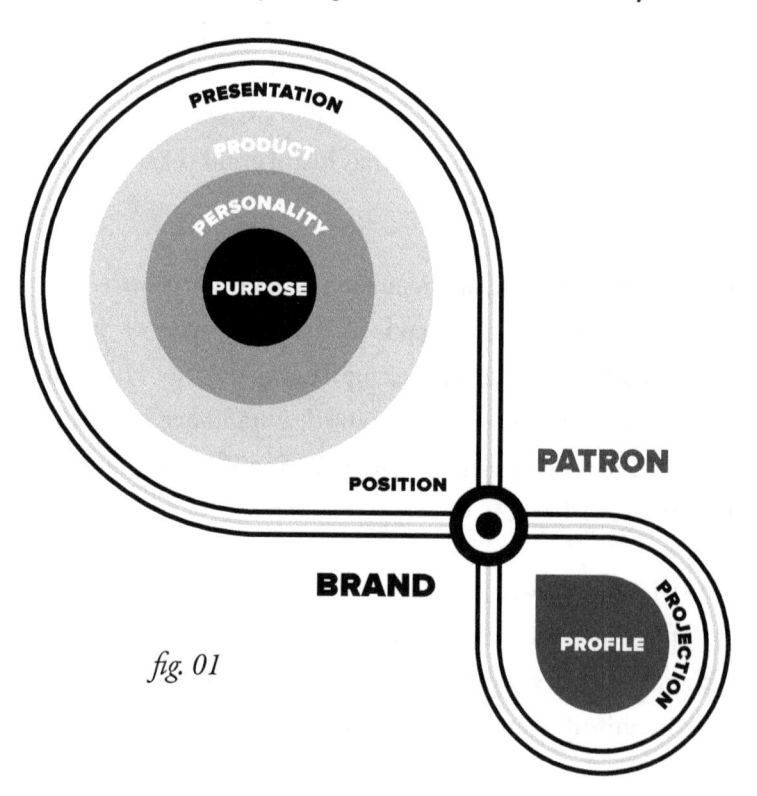

fig. 01

the components of a brand and their relationship. The fruits of this endeavor are shown here, and lovingly labeled, The Golden Lasso (figure 01).

We didn't call it that because we adore Wonder Woman. It's another handy bull pun of which there are many in this book. Despite the fun pun, The Golden Lasso is a perfect description of the diagram as it illustrates the real purpose of branding as a discipline and endeavor: to create unbreakable bonds between the brand and the people they look to attract, their Patron.

Understanding the meaning and purpose behind each component in the brand infrastructure will help you in the process of building your brand. None of these components should be undermined or taken lightly because collectively they create a full understanding of the interdependent and influential inner workings of a bullhearted brand.

Furthermore, this diagram isn't a frivolous workstream to tick the box of strategy. The most effective strategies are the ones that are used and activated. Once you have the insights afforded by The Golden Lasso, you will use it to make brand-altering decisions across every discipline inside and outside the restaurant—from marketing to operations, human resources to philanthropy.

With that, let's unpack the components of The Golden Lasso and a top-level understanding of what each of them represents. We'll dive into the fuller understandings of each throughout the remainder of the book.

Patron: Your brand's best friends

Just as humans have a group of people they gravitate towards, brands do too. Patrons are a definable group of people that the brand is being built, or evolved, to attract as their primary fans. Additionally, the Patron profile should consider the people inside the organization and their personality traits. They will be the ones guiding the experience day-to-day, top to bottom, so they must have the brand's values baked into their core.

To get a full view of the desired Patron, we excavate demographic and behavioral data that gets distilled into a detailed overview. That overview outlines the details of who this Patron is, their brand choices, and the values and perceptual needs that drive those decisions. But demographic data isn't enough to understand the Patron's drivers, so we bifurcate the definition into two parts: the demographic Profile and the Projection layer.

Profile

A Patron's profile will be familiar to anyone that's taken a marketing 101 course. It outlines the demographic information from age, sex, race, household income, and other metrics that paint a picture of the literal information about a person and group. This information is critical to locating pockets where these groups flourish for locations research, marketing research, and other marketing tactics.

Projection

The Project layer is a unique element of our process. This layer taps into the behaviors and values of the Patron which drives their brand curation practices. By looking at behavioral data mixed with purchasing behavior, we develop a clear vision of the values the Patron looks to project to the world around them. This knowledge is critical since your brand is seeking to become one of the ones the Patron adopts into their life.

Purpose: Your reason for being

This platform is the heartbeat of your brand—your true north. Your Purpose is your entire reason for being. It's how you wish to make a ding in the universe. We will spend a lot of time discussing how to excavate this purpose and how to build the brand around this as the epicenter later in the book. The purpose is the "Why" of the brand.

Personality: Your brand's unique values and traits

Your brand's personality is extremely important as it dictates the look, feel, and tone of voice you put into the world. This directly affects the visual identity, interior environment, and general attitude of the brand experiences. Outside of the Presentation layer elements, the Personality should also affect your product mix, operational procedures, and every other part of the brand. This is crucial for creating a believable statement about who you are. The Personality is the "How" of your brand.

Product: What you do and how you do it

When you hear the word "product," most likely your mind jumps to the food. This is partially correct. Your brand's product also encompasses the method of service, procedures, and the other tangible things. The product is the "What" of your brand, and it should be crafted through the lens of the Purpose and the Personality.

Presentation: How you present yourself to your Patrons

Normally when one discusses "branding," the Presentation layer's elements are what come to mind. Logos, interior design, and the various other visual aspects of a brand experience comprise what we call the Presentation layer. And while on its own, the Presentation does not constitute true "branding," it is an important and highly recognizable component. When driven by Purpose, Personality, and Product, the Presentation layer performs a powerful role: To present the brand's distinct offering to Patrons in a way that's unique, noticeable, and remarkable.

Position: Where you exist in the Patron's world

It's important to understand what makes your restaurant different compared to the competition. In this way, you can help build strong points of differentiation that help the consumer base categorize their minds. Additionally, this directly fuels ideas and angles for successful marketing efforts. The entire brand side of the lasso must be influenced by its position in the market. That requires a discerning eye and honest approach to evaluating the brand's platforms to ensure they are unique and not a regurgitation of what's already out there. In short, effective Positioning will prevent copycatting.

This is, of course, a high-level overview of the Golden Lasso's platforms and their role in crafting the details of a brand. It's more than just a pretty picture. It is the key to building an actual brand that's primed to scale. To that end, we will dive deeper into these platforms and give you the thinking, theories, and tools to build a bullhearted brand that's primed to charge ahead.

Getting Started with the Right Mindset

At first blush, the Golden Lasso may seem simple, after all, that's the point of good informational design. But its mechanics and platforms are more complex. Each platform affects the others in profound ways, making it very difficult to find a starting point if you're without a sherpa. Good news, I'm your sherpa!

Chances are you have some basic vision of the kind of restaurant you want to create. At the very least you probably have homed in on a cuisine and general format—something like, "a fast-casual pizza like Blaze Pizza, but with better ingredients." That's a great place to start with one major caveat: You have to be ready to change it based on the research and knowledge you gain in this book and in this process. Do not hammer that square peg into a round hole just because you're married to the idea.

The extensive nature of building a bullhearted brand excavates new data and information that must be absorbed and evaluated against preconceived ideas and visions of what this restaurant will be or turn into (if you're engaging in a rebranding workstream.) Therefore, we suggest you take a page out of Bruce Lee's book and be like water:

> Be like water making its way through cracks. Do not be assertive, but adjust to the object, and you shall find a way around or through it. If nothing within you stays rigid, outward things will disclose themselves.
>
> Empty your mind, be formless. Shapeless, like water. If you put water into a cup, it becomes the cup. You put water into a bottle and it becomes the bottle. You put it in a teapot, it becomes the teapot. Now, water can flow or it can crash. Be water, my friend.[4]

---

[4] Bruce Lee, *Striking Thoughts: Bruce Lee's Wisdom for Daily Living* (Tokyo: Tuttle Publishing, 2002).

What I mean by that is to be adaptable and be ready and prepared for change. When you excavate new information, allow it to be absorbed and empower yourself to adjust your original thinking based on the new knowledge. Let go of the preconceptions and embrace a stronger idea and direction.

With that as a basis, it's time to dig in. So, where do you begin?

We suggest you start by assigning the components of your current vision to their appropriate platforms in the diagram. If your vision is as stated in the example above, it belongs in the Product platform. Type out that product information in as much detail as you have available, then leave it there. Clear your mind of it.

Now that you've offloaded your current vision, you can jump into the process. We suggest starting with identifying your Patron, and, therefore, the next chapter focuses on exactly that.

3. People Power Brands

Bull Story: 95-96 Chicago Bulls

The Story

The 1995–96 NBA season was one for the record books for the Chicago Bulls. That season saw the Bulls set the record for most wins in an NBA regular season finishing with 72 wins and 10 losses. The Bulls' started 37–0 at home, part of a 44 game winning streak including games from the previous season. Their 33 road wins were the most in NBA history. The season was the best 3-loss start in NBA history at 41–3 (.932), which included an 18-game winning streak for the team. The Bulls became the first NBA team to ever win 70 regular season games, finishing first overall in their division, conference, and the entire NBA. They are also the only team in NBA history to win more than 70 games and an NBA title in the same season. Michael Jordan and Scottie Pippen were both selected for the 1996 NBA All-Star Game, as Jordan led the league in scoring with 30.4 points per game, while Phil Jackson was named Coach of The Year and was selected to coach the Eastern Conference in the All-Star Game.

That is a lot of accolades for one team in one season, and there are many factors that came together to form this perfect storm. Steve

3. People Power Brands

Kerr who is now the coach of the Golden State Warriors recalled the season this way:

> It was one of those years where everything went right. There was incredible motivation; and everything clicked. As motivated as Michael [Jordan] always was, that year was another few degrees higher based on what he had been through, the absence from the game, the loss the previous year to Orlando. The motivation was just incredible. It carried on the entire season, and that's what made it so remarkable. That was all part of it in training camp and the mode he set, the competition level in the scrimmages and the practices; he set the bar really high and he was ferocious. That was just a byproduct of the tone he set right from the beginning.
>
> Any sort of big game that had anything special about it brought out the best in us. I remember the Houston game and they had Barkley and Hakeem and Drexler (and were defending champions) and they were going to be our equivalent in the Western Conference. We went to Houston and really took it to them (double digit win). The Lakers game when Magic came back to play and in the Forum and we hammered them (by 15), the four game sweep of Orlando (in the playoffs). That was supposed to be the clash of titans; we sweep them. It seemed like the bigger the challenge, the better that team played.[5]

The Bulls had a team full of set pieces, each amazing in their own

---

[5] Steve Kerr, quoted in "72-10: A Look Back at the Greatest Team in NBA History," NBA.com, https://www.nba.com/bulls/history/72-10,

right. Together they were nearly unstoppable. From Coach Phil Jackson to Michael Jordan, Dennis Rodman, and Steve Kerr, that Bulls team will never be forgotten.

The Lesson: People Make a Brand Unstoppable

It's not enough to get people to do a job to standard. They have to believe in the team and each other. They need to trust leadership and work as a unit. While the Chicago Bulls had Michael Jordan, it wasn't he alone that broke all those records and won the championship. It was the entire team working together that did that. The magic of that seasons' Bulls team is in the people.

The players and coaching staff weren't solely gifted in their own right; they brought out the best in each other. They had a phenomenal leader at the helm with a team of leaders around him. Together they coached amazing talent into all new heights of strength, agility, and prowess making for a team that couldn't be beaten but 10 times.

The perfect storm starts with having the right people in the right roles all firing with the same purpose in their hearts. Those people collectively create the believability and meaning in a brand and raise it to all-new levels. However, many companies don't invest in attracting the top talent necessary to win. Additionally, while they may spend some time training and onboarding, it tends to be a "set it and forget it" approach, meaning that once initial training is finished, the skills aren't developed after the fact.

Imagine if the Bulls had only practiced once or only a few times. How far would they have gone? Sure, they had primo talent, and one could presume that that talent would have taken them the whole way. But anyone who's watched sports with any kind of seriousness knows that individual talent will only take you so far. Crafting a team culture and developing synergy between each member of the team is what transforms a group of talented individuals into a powerhouse. While practice truly does make perfect, ongoing training takes things to the next level.

Branding Is not Just a Marketing Focus

As stated in the Branding Truths section, branding is not all about the visuals. It's a discipline and endeavor shared throughout every part of the organization. That includes operations, finance, franchising, and so on.

Effective branding starts at the top. It's activated downward to every internal stakeholder. Even the person scrubbing the stovetops at 3 a.m. When a brand's purpose is fully believed and lived, that brand becomes a juggernaut, a charging bull that's nearly impossible to stop. But these instances aren't the majority. Instead, we all witness shallow brands every single day.

Shallow brands can be bold paper tigers who put on a good show. They can also be obviously transparent and never make a mark in their markets. Both share the same characteristics: there is no truth behind their claims. They put the proverbial writing on the wall. They may even pay big ad dollars to get their messages seen, but when one pulls back the curtain, it's just a little old dude who's unimpressive and no threat at all.

No matter how big your advertising budget, how unique the creative, and how big the organization, bullshit is bullshit, and people will sniff it out quicker than you think.

The hallmark of a shallow brand is in the prevalent thinking that branding is marketing's job and only marketing's job. Operations can't be bothered by marketing, so they focus on what they know, making processes easier, systems optimized, and a laser focus on consistency. While those focuses are great, they miss one element critical to building a strong brand experience: Why?

Why is that the product mix? Why those ingredients? Why are things done that way? What's the end goal, and what's the purpose driving those decisions?

A restaurant brand that operates and makes operational choices without brand understanding and purpose, is a ticking time bomb. Menus get overcrowded with "fat," quality of product decreases, and the level of service flails out of control. Without reason or purpose, processes don't get followed. Purpose adds value and respect for a common goal.

The same can be said about every other discipline within a restaurant organization from board level down. Without a knowledge and full understanding of the brand's reason for existence, the brand will never reach its full potential. And full potential has some beautiful benefits like lower employee turnover, higher sales and traffic comps, and a following that builds with ever-growing momentum.

So, no, branding is not solely a marketing thing, and as a leader, you need to believe this truth. Let's dig deeper into that.

Good Leader, Bad Leader

I have seen many types of CEOs and presidents, spanning from the highly experienced veteran who's indelibly convinced of their expertise and greatness, to the visionary who can't focus long enough to activate a full thought. And, yes, I've definitely seen some brilliant leaders who marched their teams and brands forward into greatness. These leaders, good and bad, have a number of things in common.

Bad leaders surround themselves with meager, timid underlings there to do the leader's bidding without question. While they may have expertise and knowledge, it pales in comparison to the grandeur and majesty of the fearless leader's.

Bad leaders refuse outside advice and information relying solely on their own gut and knowledge. Even in the face of oblivion, bad leaders do not admit defeat, and they don't identify the areas to change to avoid it. They are bull-headed (not hearted) and will go down the ship with all of their unwavering pride.

Bad leaders are slow to evolve—if they ever evolve. They don't change with the times because they don't recognize changing times as viable, valuable, or anything more than passing trends. Instead, they stick to their my-way-or-the-highway mentalities while their restaurant brand rots into irrelevance.

Bad leaders build a culture of negative reinforcement and fear. They rule with iron fists. They're unable to attract top talent, or, if they do, they don't keep it for long.

Good leaders are gems. They make everyone around them stronger, smarter, and better. They empower their people to not just perform better but think better and more effectively. Under the guidance of a great leader, brands attract top talent from top to bottom.

Good leaders understand culture and its power in driving brands ahead. They foster and nurture a positive, yet stern, environment, where people can grow and realize the potential in themselves, their responsibilities, and the brand in which they grow.

Good leaders embrace brand thinking, then work tirelessly to onboard it throughout their teams. They empower their leadership team to do the same, who continue that endeavor until every corner of the stakeholder suite "gets it." They understand the power of purpose and the power purpose brings to every job function and every team member.

Good leaders are the key to effective, successful branding, and in turn, the success of the company as a whole.

In order to create a successful brand and launch a successful branding initiative, you must be a good leader. You must understand your role and the role you play in nurturing the brand's system throughout the organization. You must be ready to make hard choices and have hard conversations because any weakness in the brand is a weakness that diminishes the brand's chances of sustained success.

Who Will Champion This Brand?

Brands don't take hold on their own. If a strategy is created but never activated, it does nothing at all. Therefore, the purpose of leadership is to be the ultimate champion of the brand's vision and ideals. However, it doesn't start and stop at the top. It has to be activated from top to bottom. That means that the Board and CEO must be completely bought in on the strategy and understand the need for it to be completely activated across all channels and opportunities.

But leadership buy-in isn't enough to garner full buy-in and understanding throughout the organization. After all, how much connectivity does a CEO have with a line cook who works the late shift? Yet, that line cook is integral in realizing the gold standard brand experience, and therefore, must understand their role in that realization.

You need to identify and empower Brand Champions.

A brand champion is someone who has fully absorbed the brand's strategy and details to the point where they understand what it means and what it looks like in action. They should be a cheerleader who can uplift, inspire, and empower the people around them. Brand champions are the key to fully realizing a brand strategy in companies large and small.

The number of champions you need depends on the size of the company. If you're a small, one-unit restaurant, a couple of champions in addition to leadership will work. If you're a larger organization, you'll need many more. Full buy-in from as many people as possible is the goal so you really cannot have too many champions.

How do you identify a candidate for brand championing?

Brand Champions have a few characteristics that we already mentioned, but there are a few more. They're charismatic and energetic. They are unafraid to challenge people's actions and methods with the understanding that adjustments are for the greater good of the brand. They get excited about the brand's purpose and fully understand the components/platforms of the restaurant's brand strategy. Brand champions should have trust from their team to a degree equivalent to their position.

Every organization has people who are primed for championing the brand. You need to find them, then equip and empower them with the knowledge and vision they need to start to own the brand. But this isn't about being highly prescriptive like an operational process. It's more about giving them the groundwork and guidance for them to start to own it in a way that is simultaneously on-brand and in their own way. It's a balance, but an important one, because if things are too prescriptive, they'll fall flat and inauthentic, creating disbelief in the Patron.

Who Are Your Brand's Stakeholders?

The most common answer you'll hear about a brand's stakeholders is the consumer. Some call them a target market or audience; some have more clever names. Most focus solely on those who will buy your food and frequent your restaurant. This myopic view removes many other stakeholders that play critical roles in your restaurant's operations and existence.

For instance, at the time of this writing, labor is a hot-button issue. Skilled, engaged staff are scarce and the effort to attract them is as competitive as marketing to consumers. Newsflash: employees, current and potential, are stakeholders. They aren't a means to an end, or simply the cogs in the machine. Engaged and dedicated labor is a valuable thing, and your brand's ability to attract that talent is crucial. Yet, many brands across every industry fail to realize this and solely focus their brand-building efforts on the customer. Big mistake.

Your stakeholder group doesn't stop with the employees either. It goes deeper into more layers of folks inside and outside of the organization from board members to sourcing partners and everything in between. Despite the array of various disciplines and roles your Patron group may play, they should all be united in the brand's foundations and should share an understanding of the core Patron and its multiple layers.

The core Patron group is the representation of the brand's focus. It's from this group that we want to attract consumers and employees. If they live, love, and represent our brand effectively, they solidify a sound foundation for growth. So, let's talk about them in more depth.

Patron: Identifying and Understanding Your Best Friends

When we ask restaurateurs who their "audience" is, we get the same response nearly every time: everyone. This is delusional thinking that's rebutted by many adages and sayings. The most famous is by Stephen Herfst: "By being everything to everyone you're nothing to anyone."[6] And yet, the common desire by most entrepreneurs and businesspeople is to market to everyone.

Generalist brands think they have an advantage by appealing to everyone and not committing fully in any one direction. They are

---

6 Stephen Herfst, "Stephen Herfst Quotes," Goodreads, accessed April 13, 2021, https://www.goodreads.com/quotes/516293-by-being-everything-to-everyone-you-re-nothing-to-anyone.

wrong. You can't have everyone love your brand because everyone is different and seek out different values. They tend to gravitate towards tribes or subcultures and look for brands that add weight to their projected selves. A generalist brand doesn't add value or believability to that attaché because their brand is vanilla. This makes these types of restaurant brands easily forgotten and hard to position in the consumer's mind. More often than not, these types of brands don't make it onto a Patron's radar at all.

Marketing everything to everyone is extremely costly, and rare is the case where it's done effectively. Chances are, you don't have the kind of budget to create well-funded, effective marketing campaigns for countless audiences and numerous foods. So, let's stop with the delusion that everyone will love your restaurant, and anyone can find something they love, and let's home in on who your Patrons truly are.

Your core Patron has a mix of three elements: Prominence, Poised, and Influence. It's important to be a mix of those three and not one and only one. Your core Patron must be prominent in your market but does not necessarily have to be the most prominent group. They should be poised to love your brand—meaning your brand should be uniquely aligned with their values and desires. Finally, they should be influential. That means they should be able to introduce the brand to others.

Finding a group of people with all three doesn't mean other groups are off-limits. The more you know about your potential customers, the more powerful your brand can become. That said, your brand's messaging and communications should be hyper-focused on fostering the love and buy-in from that core audience. Refrain from muddying the waters trying to attract them all. If you've done the job of effectively identifying your core Patron, all energy should be focused on getting them to love your brand.

Knowing your core Patron is way more detailed than simply knowing their demographic information. The key to fostering that love is found in all the layers of your core Patron. Let's dive into what those layers are and why they matter.

The Multiple Layers of Patrons

Patron groups have two layers to them. There is the statistical information like age, race, religion, household income, and sex that formulates the Profile layer. This is the information most people research and focus energy on identifying. While it has its benefits, without the second layer in full view, building a brand and marketing it is difficult and risky.

The Projection layer may be the most important layer of the Patron. This layer identifies the perceptions a patron desires from the world around them. It explains why some people choose one brand over another, and why two similar products can have vastly different audiences.

Profile Layer: Who they are

This is the collection of data that most people are familiar with when identifying a "target market" or "audience." It's the culmination of hard demographic data like age range, gender percentages, and household income. Some even pull in behavioral data like affinity brands, shopping habits, and other actions that further define the consumer.

The Patron's profile layer is still important because the data helps brands identify where their core Patrons geographically exist. With the ability to identify where they are en masse, brands can plan out growth strategies for new locations and new markets with a certain amount of confidence.

When you're developing the Profile layer of your Patron, we suggest pulling data from as many sources as you can. If you're already in operation, your website analytics and social media reporting can give you a very good understanding of your Patron based on actual data. Additionally, a lot of online ordering systems and CRM systems provide data you can use to get a full few of your customer's demographic information.

Outside of owned digital marketing analytics and reports, there are other tools out there to farm data based on zip codes and neighborhoods. A simple Google search will bring up many options. One of our favorites is Esri's tapestry search. This system has been invaluable in finding core patron groups across the nation.

Having a clear understanding of who your Patron is from a demographic and behavioral perspective gives you powerful knowledge upon which you can guide operational and marketing decisions. But this isn't the end-all be-all. You need to understand what motivates your Patrons.

Projection Layer: Why they buy

Projected traits are what motivates people to choose one brand over another. They represent how patrons want to be viewed by the world. As a result, they drive purchase decisions as every person chooses brands based on what that brand represents.

We know this is a reality because of the sheer volume of viable, competing brands that sell virtually the same product. If it did not exist, we'd all be driving the same car, same color, same model. Instead, we have choices, and those choices aren't solely features and price-based. There's much more to the purchase decision in addition to objective factors.

People select brands that represent their values and personality. When you build a brand to stand for something, or multiple things, that brand becomes representative of those traits. Those traits are what people look for and essentially buy.

For instance, Apple represents forward-thinking design, so when one purchases an Apple product they absorb that trait into their projected self. When someone sees that person with their Apple, that person is associated with "forward-thinking design." People make their choices with this in mind, which culminates into a curated suite of brands that project their desired personality to the world.

In practice, it looks something like this: My friend Lauren wears LuluLemon athleisurewear. She drives a new Prius and shops exclusively at Whole Foods. She has a membership to OrangeTheory and can be found every morning at her local Starbucks. She works at a nonprofit that seeks to plant more trees in urban areas.

Without telling you anything objectively about Lauren, you have learned enough to formulate a view of her and what she stands for simply by learning her brand choices. I could tell you that Lauren never uses her OrangeTheory membership, doesn't work out, eats junk food, and rarely recycles, and that wouldn't change your perceptions of her. The brands she has chosen to adopt communicate her values despite her actions.

These projected traits are powerful elements of the human psyche. Often we do not recognize what we're doing. We're simply drawn to some brands over others, but know that our desired projections are what's driving that.

If you need any more convincing, consider the power of Instagram and the influencer revolution. Instagram tapped the vanity nerve for millions of people around the world, but it wasn't just pictures of them smiling or hanging with their dog. Frequently pictures were taken at places, buying things, frequenting brands, etc. All of this drove at developing a view of who that person is whether or not it was true. After all, we all have heard of the jet one can rent to take photos in to look like a baller. In case you haven't, here you go: https://nymag.com/intelligencer/2017/10/you-can-rent-a-grounded-private-jet-to-take-instagram-photos.html

The Patron Most Brands Forget

Companies and consultants spend copious amounts of time identifying their perfect patrons. Whether it's at the beginning of the journey, during growth, or looking to evolve, understanding your patron is critical to realizing success. However, the patrons with whom you're seeking to foster love are only one of a few groups. And of the other patrons, the ones that matter most are your internal Patrons.

The internal Patron profile covers the people who are primed to be fantastic team members for your brand. You can't focus on age, sex, race, identity, or other discriminatory categories (and why should you?) So the focus is on their behaviors and their values in general. Every brand wants hardworking, dedicated team members, but what about their culture and attitude? If that doesn't align, then you're crippling and deteriorating the brand experience where it matters most: on the inside.

Although it may seem counterintuitive, successful businesses require many different types of team members. Whether it's a highly organized, procedural-minded maverick or an energetic, bubbly go-getter, it takes multiple types of skill sets to make the machine work. That said, skill sets and demographic categories aren't the best way to attract strong team members. What matters most is cultural alignment.

Finding cultural alignment starts with making your brand's culture abundantly clear across the brand's marketing and communications. Culture isn't something you say, it's something everyone else experiences. When done effectively, it attracts both external and internal patrons en masse. In order to establish and foster that culture, you need to have a fully realized understanding of your brand (probably why you're reading this book.) From there, messaging, communications, design, and everything else work collectively to build believability in the brand as a whole. And that's the first step in attracting team members who align.

Establishing the brand across the owned channel ecosystem is important, but not enough to attract the talent. You have to woo them. You have to court them and draw them in. You have to advertise to them with the full mix of paid and owned media just as you would with a limited-time offer or other marketing initiative.

Working for your brand should be exhilarating for anyone aligned on the cultural and personality level. Marketing to them should focus on that dynamic before delivering the objective information like salaries and benefits. Put creative energy into the advertising from job descriptions through every media outlet's visual presentation of the brand.

Finally, although hiring is a human resources ask, identifying the right cultural fit does require that your HR professionals completely understand the brand's strategy and platforms. After all, how do they know a candidate is the right fit if they don't thoroughly know the brand? It'd be impossible. Therefore, onboarding your HR manager or team with the brand's strategy and Patron's profile data is an important step forward in building that rockstar level team.

In Real Life: How a Sustainable Brand Fails to Sustain its People

Never in my short life have I heard about any other brand more than Chipotle when it comes to restaurant strategy, branding, etcetera. For years now, that brand has been either mentioned and/or discussed in every new business interaction, even after the business has been won. And it's with good reason.

Chipotle took the nation by storm about a decade ago with a refreshing upgrade to the typical QSR experience. From elevated food through a refreshingly cool interior experience, Chipotle rapidly gained followers and with them, revenue. In parallel, the brand caught the eyes of every restaurateur and food-focused visionary who was energized by what the fast-casual format could become. And so, "the Chipotle of …" phrasing to a majority of pitches and concept descriptions took hold and grew.

3. People Power Brands

The brand's rapid rise to fame and fortune was a testament to the power of true branding. Chipotle built its brand on one word: sustainability. From the food to the buildouts, sustainable food made accessible and affordable to the masses upped the fast-food game nearly overnight. It wasn't only because "sustainability" was, and quite possibly still is, a buzzword. It was because they truly meant it.

With every facet of the brand, sustainability was the driving decision maker. Sourcing focused on sustainable food and food ecosystems. The preparation line adopted a manufacturing process to make all levels of traffic sustainable. The list goes on. But Chipotle missed one area with its sustainable mantra: its people.

Over the last few years, Chipotle has experienced multiple bouts of strikes and protests.[7] From increases in minimum wage through demands for sick leave and other benefits,[8] Chipotle workers have felt disenfranchised by the brand. As I've already outlined clearly, a brand's people are its most critical asset in delivering believability in the brand's promises. If the people are mad, the brand will suffer, and Chipotle is not immune.

When people see Chipotle's workers striking, a message is sent. While the brand may be all about sustainability, they are not ensuring the sustainability of their team members. And that lack

---

[7] u/Wowawewahwah, "NYC Chipotle Workers on Strike," *Reddit*, March 5, 2020, https://www.reddit.com/r/Chipotle/comments/fdyuwb/nyc_chipotle_workers_on_strike/.

[8] Naomi LaChance, "Chipotle Workers Walk Out Over Labor Complaints," Splinter, September 24, 2019, https://splinternews.com/chipotle-workers-walk-out-over-labor-complaints-1838424946; Sydney Pereira, "Chipotle Workers Demand Company Comply with Sick Leave Laws Amid Covid-19 Outbreak," **gotham**ist, March 6, 2020, https://gothamist.com/news/chipotle-workers-demand-company-comply-sick-leave-laws-amid-covid-19-outbreak.

of alignment speaks loudly for the believability in Chipotle's brand promises, creating a fissure in the brand's credibility. And that fissure, when left unaddressed and unfixed, can easily become a crack, then an insurmountable chasm.

Now, I'm sure Chipotle will be fine, but that's not the question. The question is could they be better? Could they take their already impressive market dominance and raise the bar to all new levels? If they took their sustainability brand passion and applied it to the human resources world, they could establish a new paradigm for restaurants: the teams that make them succeed, and the relationship between the two.

4. Positioning for Success

Bull Story: Javanese Bull

The Story

The Sumatrans have a legend about a bullfight.[9] The Javanese attempted to conquer Sumatra so they could take control of their rich fertile farming land. Rather than fight an unwinnable war, the West Sumatrans proposed that they settle the land dispute with a bullfight. The Javan king accepted the proposal, knowing he had many fine bulls. Victory was inevitable. And so the Javans returned home to select their finest bull and took it to West Sumatra to fight with the West Sumatrans' prize bull.

Meanwhile, realizing their people could never find a bull as large as the Javanese, one clever West Sumatran had an idea that would be an unexpected proposal.

The West Sumatrans fielded a baby bull with V-shaped knives attached to its horns. The horns gave the impression of a small, helpless bull in comparison to the Javans' immense specimen. When the Javan bull was put into the bull ring, it was very surprising to see a small baby calf as an opponent.

---

[9] "Sumatran Legends," Sumatra-Indonesia.com, updated July 20, 2008, http://www.sumatra-indonesia.com/sumatralegends.htm.

Once the fight started, the baby bull perceived its opponent as its mother and rushed to suckle the Javanese bull. In the process of seeking the udder, the calf ripped out the bull's belly, winning the fight and the wager. While the West Sumatrans feasted on the conquered bull, the Javanese quickly retreated back to Java allowing the West Sumatrans to keep their land.

The Lesson: Respect Thy Competition

How did the Javanese lose? They had might, and they had the fight in the bag. They lost because they did not respect their opponents. Their lack of respect rendered them unable and unwilling to conceive a world where they'd lose or how that could happen. Hubris isn't only an ugly quality, it's a crippling one.

Far too often restaurants have little, or only basic, knowledge of their competitors. They are so convinced that those competitors are subpar and so enamored with their own concept, they never think to invest the time to scrutinize what makes them great and popular. They say things like, "Our food is superior to theirs! It's so good that once people try it, they won't go back!" The hubris runs thick, and they never see the baby calf's sharp knives coming for their belly.

If that thinking is flipped, the story and opportunity shift in favor of the brand and restaurateur, not the competition. The key to flipping the scenario is respect and understanding.

Victors have respect for their competitors and work to understand their strengths. Rather than relying on superficial or anecdotal knowledge or passing competitors off as subpar, successful leaders thoroughly analyze them and develop a rich understanding of strengths and weaknesses. Through thorough analysis, one can find the weak spots in any prize bull. There is, after all, a chink in every armor.

Finding those weak spots is the goal of successful positioning endeavors, and positioning is an absolute must for every successful restaurant brand. The world does not need another pizza brand (although we love pizza.) However, it may need a pizza brand that brings something new to the table.

A lack of understanding of a brand's position leaves its belly vulnerable to the calf's blades. In this setup, the calf is the competition. Be it a large, existing brand, or a young and hungry startup, strong positioning is critical to continued brand success.

Why Positioning Still Matters

Positioning is not a new concept and many books have been written on the topic. The most famous and well-respected book is arguably *Positioning: The Battle for your Mind*. In that book, the duo of Al Ries and Jack Trout define positioning as "an organized system for finding a window in the mind. It is based on the concept that communication can only take place at the right time and under the right circumstances."[10]

Their theory still holds true, but it has gotten exponentially more complex as the complexity of humans has advanced so far. Think about it. At the advent of television and throughout its first few decades, programs were simple 30-minute spurts of entertainment found on one of three available channels. The programs' stories

---

[10] Al Ries and Jack Trout, Positioning: The Battle for Your Mind (New York: McGraw-Hill, 2001), 19.

began and ended within that 30-minute window, except for the notable "to be continued..." double episode formats. And for a while, that worked.

As time marched on, people became more complex and demanded more from entertainment. Movies became available to watch at home. The core three networks were joined by other channels that homed in on categories and niche entertainment topics. This expansion continues today, and we have actually shifted into a new paradigm where people are empowered to be selective of not only which channels they watch but the ones they choose to subscribe to. We have come so far as a species and society that we've realized an awesome level of customized selection that's tailored quite closely to who we are and who we want to be. And entertainment isn't the only arena where this expansion of choice has been experienced and realized.

To date, there are nearly 100 models of automobiles manufactured in the United States.[11] A simple stroll through a supermarket will see one bombarded by brands and products from monk fruit sweetener to kumquats, all with private label alternatives. If that's not enough, imagine the vast array of items for sale on websites like Amazon and Wayfair. Suffice to say, we have options for everything, but why?

We have options because as a species and society we have advanced our thinking and societal representation needs to levels beyond imagination. We're connected with others from around the world

---

[11] "List of Automobiles Manufactured in the United States, Wikipedia, last modified March 26, 2021, https://en.wikipedia.org/w/index.php?title=Special:CiteThisPage&page=List_of_automobiles_manufactured_in_the_United_States&id=1014316091&wpFormIdentifier=titleform.; Kelsey Mays, "The Cars.com 2020 American-Made Index: Which Cars are Most American?" Cars.com, June 23, 2020, https://www.cars.com/articles/the-cars-com-2020-american-made-index-which-cars-are-most-american-422711/.

and down the street at the tap of an app button, and with that connectivity comes the need to separate oneself from the pack. The need for individualism is as strong as the need for collectivism. More accurately, there exists a need in individuals to simultaneously feel connected and unique within a collective. We all want to feel included in groups, but unique within them. And that's the core of why positioning is effective and still matters.

In the Industrial era, a company simply needed to throw up a name on a shingle, and boom, you're in business. During this era, you'd see very utilitarian company names like The Ford Motor Company or Grandma Betty's Biscuit Powder. The approach to advertising was based on features and benefits. A good product at a good price was the key to success.

Fast forward to today and things have drastically shifted. Today, that setup isn't enough to succeed. In fact, "good price" is relatively irrelevant. I mean, you can buy a purse for $30,000 USD, and it carries the same stuff just as well as a purse that comes at a more approachable price point. So, what's the magic sauce then? In one word, positioning.

Positioning in today's reality is a mix of multiple brand components, price and product being one of them. A brand's offering consists of a purpose, personality, product, and how it presents itself to the world in a way that's positioned to uniquely and effectively attract a core patron. It's not enough to have a good product or the mix of good product, good service, at a good price. People demand more substance and more attributes that help them categorize the brand in their life, which is jammed with millions of brands and messages.

Therefore, positioning, when done correctly, places the brand in the mind of the consumer with nuances and details that serve as "tags." That information manifests in definitive statements and/or beliefs: "This brand is for people like me" or "this brand is not for people like me." Your brand will have people in both camps, and that's okay.

Each of us is bombarded every day with brands and messages vying for attention. The options on every shelf are plentiful, and this has resulted in the need for clear points of differentiation on multiple levels beyond utilitarian checkboxes. Now, more than ever before, positioning is absolutely critical to effective brand strategy and communications.

Competition Is a Good Thing; Learn to Love It

Age-old wisdom and the driving force behind Darwin's theory of evolution, pits you against others with the intent of prevailing; becoming the top dog (or bull.) It's in our nature to attempt to best others. It's a powerful motivator that drives ideation, determination, and the bravery to take risks. This driving force is at the heart of every entrepreneur and restaurateur, but it's important to harness it in an ethical manner and not let it get out of control.

An out of control competitive driver would lead one to look to take down competition. Sweep the leg as in the movie the Karate Kid. Why strive to be better, when you can make your competitor worse? And if you can do both, that's the magic sauce, right? Wrong. A rising tide raises all ships and nothing could be truer in the restaurant world.

The most important driver of restaurant success is getting people through the door. That starts with being in places where people already are in high numbers. It takes a compelling offer to lure them in and the ability to get people to become aware, notice, and absorb that offer. Sure, you can attempt to do that on your own by dropping a significant amount of marketing dollars on educating Patrons on your location, but you need that money for educating them on other aspects of your brand. That is unless you have an endless supply of capital, in which case, can we be best friends?

Instead, competing restaurants have a common goal on a number of different levels. Level one is collectively attracting mass amounts of foot traffic to the immediate area. Getting potential patrons to the doorsteps is a lot easier together than going it alone. Collectively, restaurants and retailers create a draw to bring people to the area. Once there, it becomes a positioning and product layer game to convert them to a dining moment. In short, does your brand jive with their vibe, and do you offer the food they crave?

The synergies between competing restaurants go beyond the traffic driving need. Competition is a sign of concept viability, which is why many investors across industries shy away from companies that claim to have zero competition. It's a dead giveaway that the company is destined for failure.

I have seen this play out in real life. An enterprising restaurateur has a vision to bring a product that works in another part of the world to the streets of Anytown USA. "People love this food in this other country and eat it all day every day, so Americans just need to try it and they'll love it, too!" says that little visionary voice in their head. Finding opportunities where others do not is an inherently unique trait that separates successful entrepreneurs from hobbyists, but in the restaurant space, this can be a danger zone.

Competition in the market is an indicator that people have already been introduced to a product, and they don't need to be educated on the details and encouraged to try it. After all, getting someone to try something new is actually quite difficult. We're creatures of habit, and we tend to go with what we know. New is scary. I'll dive into this more in the next chapter as we tackle the Product layer of your brand. For now, let it be said and known that competing brands are a sign of viability.

The final reason why competition is a great thing is this: humans work at those competing restaurants and like all humans, they tend to get fatigued on the same old thing. Simply put, other restaurant leaders and staff are your potential Patrons. That's right, those folks will inevitably eat at your restaurants and can grow to realize a level of loyalty, especially if you're not in 100% direct competition.

You should learn to love your competitors and seek to develop a relationship deeper than pleasantries and cordial professionalism. Support each other and learn to embrace competition not as a fight, but as a collective effort with a shared goal. Together you can create a surge of traffic that will raise both their ship and yours. The benefits of that are way more palatable than sabotaging their business verbally or worse.

Your Competition Isn't What You May Think

Let's say you want to open a craft burger restaurant in a suburban neighborhood where there exists a number of restaurants. Basic deduction would guide you to listing out all of the restaurants that offer burgers and marking them as competitors. And that wouldn't necessarily be a bad move. However, your actual competition very well may be broader and more nuanced than that. By homing in on the product only, you'd be missing several variables that drive decision-making by your Patron.

First, it's important to realize that you're fighting for a share of stomach. As a result, you are partially competing against the Patron's ability to prepare their own meal at home. Yes, your Patron can actually be your competition. Additionally, you're competing against everywhere else there exists food and sustenance. That includes grocery stores, convenience stores, and grandma's house. (The absolute gall of grandma to compete with your restaurant! How dare she!)

That amount of competition is overwhelming, to say the least. If you embark on attempting to identify, research, and analyze that large swath of competitive information, you'll be dead before you finish. Instead, it's critical to drill down into the details that categorize competing brands as direct competitors. Rather than pinpointing everyone and every business that makes a burger, it's easier and more effective to use geography and product details to home in on the true competition.

Continuing with our theoretical burger concept, hereto forward named Burger Queen, one could say brands like McDonald's, Burger King, Wendy's, Five Guys, Shake Shack, Steak N' Shake, and more are all competitors. Even the diner down the street that sells burgers alongside 75 other items is competing for that burger moment. When one takes a step back, however; it becomes clear that the type of people who eat at McDonald's regularly isn't really the same type who buy into Shake Shack or other higher price point fast casuals.

True competition is defined through similarities in product quality, price point, geographic availability, and sometimes Patron layer similarities. Our Burger Queen brand makes burgers from higher-end ingredients and uses multi-cultural culinary flavor profiles to create a variety of burger concoctions suited to the well-traveled and adventurous palette. Suffice to say, we're not up against Wendy's, Burger King, and McDonald's, nor is the local diner even in the same ballpark, and granny can bugger off with her basic home burgers. (Sorry, gran.)

On the product level, the competition for our theoretical Burger Queen brand is more in line with Smashburger, Grindhouse, and Farm Burger. The last two are local players in the Atlanta market, and Smashburger, although a nationwide brand, has a presence there as well. For the purposes of this example, we'll use Atlanta as the market.

Taking a step back, we've uncovered a few layers that help us home in on our brand's true competition (figure 02.) They are as follows:

Layer One: Burger-focused restaurant in the Atlanta area.

Layer Two: High-quality ingredients commanding a higher price point compared to well-known QSRs.

Layer Three: Unique burgers with multi-cultural flavor profiles.

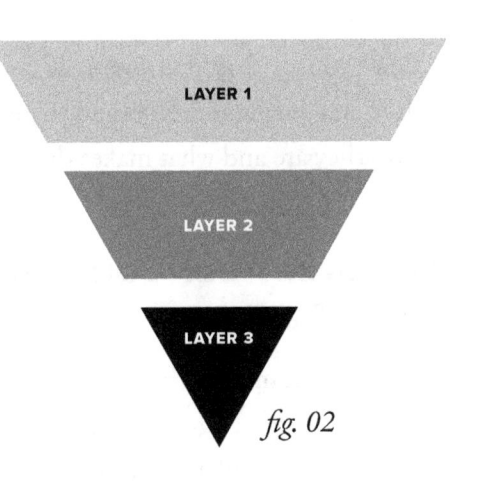

fig. 02

These three layers narrow down our competition to a set of 5-10 brands in the aforementioned market. That's a much easier group to analyze than "any place that makes a burger including grandma's house." Furthermore, the competitive analysis will get a much clearer sense of where your actual brand can dominate, or the "whitespace," as we call it.

To do this for your brand's competitive analysis workstream, ask yourself and/or your team the following questions:

1. What brands are in the immediate 3-5 mile radius of your location or locations?

2. What brands are creating food that directly competes with ours on a nuanced level?

3. Do those brands truly fight your brand for share of stomach?

4. Are these brands tapping the same Patrons we seek to attract?

Once you've identified your true competition, it's time to research the details around their brand to develop a deep understanding of who they are and what makes them tick.

Analyze Your Competition with Honesty and Clarity

The West Sumatrans from the Javanese Bull Story knew they did not have a chance going head-to-head with the Javanese bull. By studying that bull, they were able to find a way to win. They found a niche and exploited it with precision. They knew their competition and were honest about their capabilities, and it paid off. The same must be done for your brand.

Sure, you could run full-bore into launching your burrito brand because you found an awesome spot that you just fell in love with, and O-M-G have you tasted the burritos because they are the best, the absolute best, and everyone is going to love them because they're better than the other burritos that are out there. However, that'd be a recipe for disaster. In fact, I'd wage my entire life savings on failure with that scenario.

The fact is that saying and thinking that your food is the best implies that the other options out there are subpar. And while confidence is necessary to succeed and you have to believe in your own product, approaching the building and the subsequent marketing of your brand with that mentality is simply ineffective and negligent. Why? Simple, because pushing your food as the best implies that the food your Patrons already love and adore is not. Have you ever tried to tell someone they're wrong? How well does that usually go?

Let me make something very clear: You may have great food, in fact, I hope you do, otherwise, you really won't' go far. But your food is not better than what the people already love as their favorites. At least not yet. People have to come to that conclusion on their own through consistently great interactions with your brand. With each interaction, trust is built and believability is fostered. Just like any relationship.

Think about it. What do you think would happen if you walked up to a person that you found attractive and stated, "you're going to love me, I'm the best for you." Not only would you probably be laughed at, but your chances of changing their mind would be extremely disadvantageous. Of course, you think you're the best, but that holds no water when trying to convince others. So how do you convince people that your brand is worth noticing, and the food is worth trying? It starts by fully understanding who's already in that space.

You must develop a deep understanding of your competition before you open your first unit, grow in new markets, and strengthen your position in current markets. Understanding competition is the key to fine-tuning your brand and how it will attract your core Patrons.

Research and analysis beget understanding so it is my suggestion that you dive deep into the details about the brands that compete in your space. Document the brand using the same platforms used to build your own brand. Collect images of their food, façade, interiors, uniforms, advertising, essentially anything and everything you can get your hands on and print them out. Print out content from their social feeds, website, and other channels. Hang everything on the wall and absorb what you see and read with the intent of answering some critical questions:

What's their purpose? You can usually find this on the "about us" page of their website. Unfortunately, a brand's purpose stays buried instead of manifesting throughout the brand. Note, we're trying to avoid that because it's a mistake, but for you and your brand, competition that buries their purpose is a good thing.

If you had to assign personality traits, what would they be? Stick to the three most prevalent adjectives that come to mind when reviewing and analyzing the competing brands. These can be excavated by looking at how they present themselves visually and with how they write. What's their attitude?

How big are they? What's their price point? Identify how large of an organization they are by reviewing their LinkedIn company page and Wikipedia coverage. Have a dive into their menu to see where they fall with regard to pricing.

What are their strengths and weaknesses? Yeah, these are the components of the famed SWOT analysis found in traditional marketing basics. But, they still hold value and are still important. A strength is something that gives them a competitive edge or notoriety. A weakness is an area where they fall short or have received negative attention. These can spread from the food through the service and into location or even their brand identity components like a bad name or confusing advertisement.

Document your findings and presumptions thoroughly in your brand strategy plan, but don't put them away just yet. You have some more work to do to establish your brand's position. Let's charge ahead.

The Perceptual Map and How to Find Your Whitespace

Hold on, buckaroo, we're about to get real cerebral here. It's not to flex our brains and knowledge though. It really is important. If you've been following along, we've drilled down to our core, direct competitors. We then analyzed those competitors' brands from their Purpose to their positioning and everything in between. At this point, we have a deep understanding of who we're up against, but what we don't know is where there is space to compete. Where is the opportunity to establish a brand that will get noticed and draw in our Patrons?

In order to effectively position a brand's visual and verbal presentation, the whitespace must be found. This is accomplished through developing what we call a Perceptual Map (figure 03). The Perceptual Map consists of two axes with opposing attributes found in your set of competing brands. For instance, when looking at Burger Queen's, our fictional concept, competitors, we see competing attributes such as Elevated versus Basic, and Whimsical versus Craft-centric. If we plotted our competitive set on those two axes, it'd look something like this:

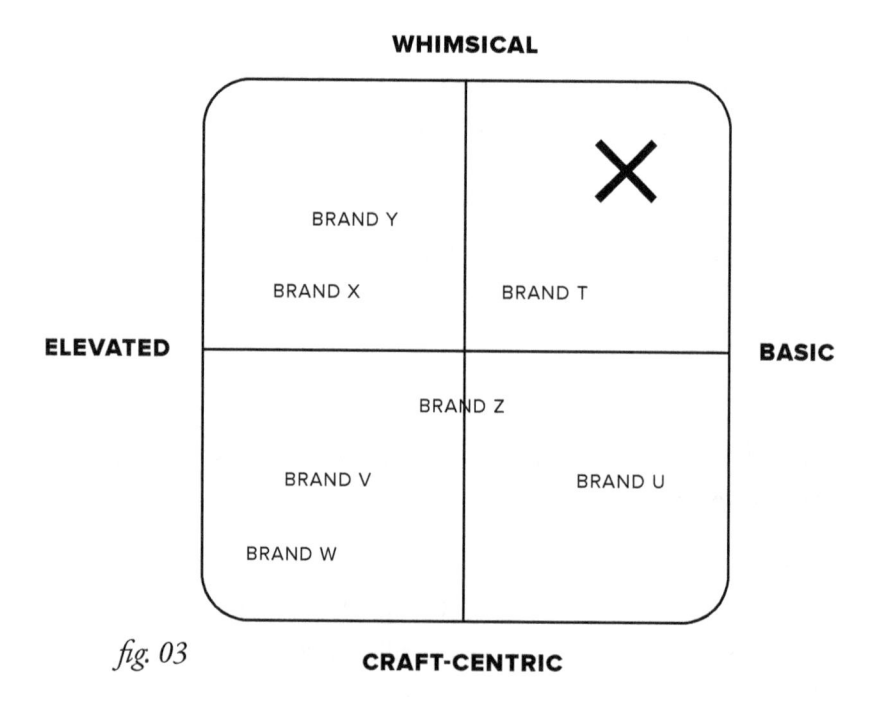

WHIMSICAL

ELEVATED — **BASIC**

BRAND Y
BRAND X
BRAND T
BRAND Z
BRAND V
BRAND U
BRAND W

fig. 03 **CRAFT-CENTRIC**

When viewing the perceptual map, it becomes abundantly clear where there are openings for our fictional concept to thrive. We call those openings the "whitespace." Whitespace offers a clear path forward for positioning the brand against the competition so the chances of being noticed and adopted by our Patrons are maximized. This is essentially the basis of Marty Neumeier's "Zag" strategy in action.[12]

Before you dive into plotting competitors and identifying your brand's whitespace, there are two rules to follow:

Rule No. 1: Axes' attributes must not be negative versus positive. Selecting where you want your brand to be on a bad versus good axis is a pretty easy task. Doing this would be lazy and ineffective. After all, no one goes into business with the intent of creating a bad experience with terrible food, and establishing that you want to be better than bad is an obvious goal. Therefore, you should be looking to identify and establish two opposing attributes. I mentioned two examples above (Whimsical vs Craft-centric, Elevated vs. Basic), but here are a few more ideas and examples:

Serious vs. Lighthearted

Historic vs. Contemporary

Rustic vs. Modern

Rule No. 2: Don't create whitespace where there is none. Perceptual Mapping can be difficult, and the inclination will be to simplify the task. But this is a critical tool in establishing the strategy of your brand, so you must avoid any shortcuts and simplifications. Put bluntly: Take this seriously.

By choosing ineffective, misaligned attributes for the axes, the opportunity to plot competitor positions hoarded in one area to

---

[12] Marty Neumeier, *Zag: The Number-One Strategy of High-Performance Brands* (Berkeley, CA: New Riders, 2007).

show a whitespace that doesn't really exist becomes inevitable. This may create a feeling of elation as you realize how big of an opportunity you have, but it's not real and destined to fail.

Finding whitespace should be a challenge. If you find it easy, you either don't have enough competitors, a really bad sign, or you've chosen the wrong axes on which to evaluate and plot. Go back to the drawing board!

Identifying and understanding your brand's whitespace empower you to finalize the connectivity between your brand and the Patron's projected values. It fuels profoundly effective communications from visual identity through verbal, advertising messaging and creative through philanthropic endeavors. It's the glue that connects the brand's components and fuels lassoing your Patrons closer to your brand in an indefatigable bond.

Effective Positioning Should Fuel Innovation

I've spent a lot of time outlining the benefits of effective positioning as they influence competitive advantages for messaging, marketing, and visual communications. There exists another benefit that has not been touched upon just yet: Innovation.

You know you've positioned your brand correctly when new ideas emerge that challenge conventions. In conjunction with the other layers of the brand strategy, positioning should open new doors and new ideas for pushing the envelope with food, service, and experience. This happens because a full understanding of your competition fuels a full understanding of your brand's uniqueness.

With that uniqueness in focus, the opportunities to reinforce it start developing.

Innovation drives the future viability of restaurant concepts. It can create a fast track to patron awareness, aiding in the growth and scale of the brand. Innovation can happen across all facets of the business as well. Whether it's a new method of outputting quantities of food or a whole new line of products, positioning should inspire ideation.

It's important to note that innovation doesn't have to be technology-focused, but technology is a major way to innovate. With the rapid adoption of technologies like third-party delivery, order-ahead and pickup, self-service kiosks, and QR code-driven experiences, the ability to push things forward are seemingly endless. However, not all innovation is effective, and there are some areas to worry about.

Just because you can, doesn't mean you should, and this adage has no greater meaning than in the context of technology-driven ideas. I've seen this play out with the introduction of new point of sale systems. Newer systems have fueled salespeople to push the idea of "virtual food halls" to customers who haven't quite thought through the details. I'll explain.

Creating names and logos can seem like an easy task. "Easy" meaning that it doesn't cost a lot of money nor does it take a lot of time. Therefore, launching a new brand has become extremely easy and turnkey with these new systems. But a name and logo are not nearly enough to create a successful brand. (Hopefully, you're picking that up by now.) Brands must be effectively marketed in order to get traction, and that takes time and budget. But that's not the only reason this is dangerous.

Categorizing brands in the mind is critical in creating successful brands. By allowing technology to guide decisions, effective categorization can be diluted at best, deteriorated at worst. This is a death blow to any brand looking to launch and/or grow.

Finally, just because a system or feature is tech-driven does not mean it's intuitive. Therefore, it's important to keep the Patron's experience where it belongs: front and center. It truly is all about them and what's going to create a smooth, intuitive experience from beginning to end, or until next time.

In Real Life: How Hubris Killed a Pizza Brand Primed to Rise Up

We love it when we're approached by a visionary leader with the guts to do something big. And that was the case when we encountered the person who was heading up a new pizza concept to launch in Atlanta. We'll call him Jack for the sake of protecting names.

Jack was hungry. He had spent countless hours over the years seeking out fantastic pizza as he pieced together his dream concept. Jack found an award-winning pizza concept and negotiated acquiring the recipe to make it the centerpiece of the offering. He even secured a reputable financier to help open, not just one location, but many over the course of five years. With the planning in place, Jack identified Atlanta as ground zero. While he surveyed location opportunities, he sought out a partner in the market to bring the concept to life. Enter Vigor.

Our interaction with Jack was one mixed with respect, energy, and an increasing level of tumult. On one hand, as a leader, Jack was empowering and encouraging, but on the other, he proved to be insulting and arrogant to a fault. The results of this persisting dichotomy were a declining interest from the team to work on the project and an increasing level of tension between both Vigor and Jack. But that's not the only place where Jack's attitude and behavior had negative effects.

Arrogance is fueled by hubris, and hubris is a deadly sin, especially when it comes to building and launching a new brand. It clouds judgment and points leaders into poor decisions across all aspects of a company. Rize's leader was plagued by hubris and it drove the company into failure. One of the more glaring examples of this trait at play was in how Jack approached relationships with competing concepts and leaders.

When coming to a new market where you have zero notoriety, influence, or history, it's critical that you make good with the players in the market. Competition isn't a bad thing. In fact, it should be embraced. The goal of any smart leader should be to develop strong relationships with the local restaurateurs and ancillary industry players. Why? Simple, they can help one steer clear of bad actors, guide toward the best areas of town, and inevitably, they'll support the business. However, if competition is approached with the goal of besting and domination, any goodwill and help will be eliminated. In the worst-case scenarios, one can easily become ostracized and boycotted, which was the case with Jack.

Here in Atlanta, we have fantastic pizza from players that we Atlantans have come to love. That doesn't mean we're not open to new pizza concepts if their vibe checks out. Rize was in a position to offer a slightly different and new experience to the Atlanta market with a pizza style that was unique. The opportunity to realize that vision crumbled quickly due to the leader's hubris and inability to see competition as a good thing.

What's Next?

So far, we have invested time in reviewing and understanding the components outside of the brand. Specifically, we have unpacked and delved into the nuances of a brand's Patron including the projection layer. From there, we jumped into the brand's position in the marketplace and how to find it. These aspects of the Golden Lasso strategy are critical steps in guiding the formation or evolution of a brand, and now that we have them fully understood and realized, it's time to turn our minds and hearts to the brand itself. Let's keep charging ahead!

5. Core Layers of a Brand

Bull Story: Ferdinand

The Story

You won't find young Ferdinand butting heads with the other bulls. He's too busy stopping under a tree to smell the flowers. That has his mom worried, but once she realizes he's happy going against the grain, she lets him be himself.

Fast forward to a grown-up Ferdinand. He's the biggest, strongest bull around, yet he's still content just smelling the flowers while all the other bulls dream of competing in Madrid's bullfights.

One day, five men come to the pasture to choose a bull for the fights. Ferdinand is again on his own, sniffing flowers, when he accidentally sits on a bee. He gets stung and runs wildly across the field, snorting and stamping. Mistaking Ferdinand for a mad, aggressive bull, the men rename him "Ferdinand the Fierce" and take him away to Madrid.

All the beautiful ladies of Madrid turn out to see the handsome matador fight "Ferdinand the Fierce." However, when Ferdinand is led into the ring, he's delighted by the flowers in the ladies' hair and lies down in the middle of the ring to enjoy them, upsetting and disappointing everyone. Ferdinand is then sent back to his pasture, where to this day, he is still smelling the flowers.

The Lesson: A Passionate Purpose Drives Everything

Written in 1936 by American author Munro Leaf, the story of Ferdinand is one of passion and purpose.[13] Ferdinand lived for a reason, a "why," and he didn't back down even when things got difficult. He stuck to what he loved. In the end, he had a long, happy life on his own terms, while the other bulls weren't so lucky.

Successful restaurant and beverage brands know who they are and why they exist. They're not afraid to be different. When they're in tough situations, they stay true to themselves. Like Ferdinand, going with the flow is never an option for a winning brand that fully lives its purpose.

Too often, brands allow the whims of trends and outside, unsupported feedback to drive their decisions. They knee-jerk react to any sign of trouble and challenges with a "gut" first approach, never considering for a moment that one's guts are full of shit. And like guts, so are unsubstantiated, directionless decisions. But what should guide decisions for a brand's path and its future? How do you know if something is the right decision for the brand? Purpose is the answer.

Every company has the same need: money. Money is the necessary gas in the tank in order to operate and grow. So much so that one could argue that money is the sole purpose of an organization. But

---

[13] Munro Leaf, *The Story of Ferdinand* (New York: Grossett & Dunlap, 2011). First Edition published in 1936 by Viking Press.

that'd be incredibly incorrect.

Businesses, especially restaurants, must be fueled by a purpose bigger than the basics of business enterprise. That purpose is a key differentiator that serves as a north star in choppy, uncharted waters. It's a sherpa and a benchmark that pulls the brand forward and pushes every person, internally and externally, towards something bigger and better.

When a restaurant makes choices based on outside influences without a means of consideration and evaluation, it becomes susceptible to wrong turns and poor choices that can cripple or kill. Ferdinand was expected to act like a bull and put up a fiery fight to the death. But it wasn't the fear of death that prevented him from following a preconceived path, it was his passion for flowers that kept him alive. He had a purpose that was clear to him. Only when he strayed did he endanger himself.

Brands must fully understand the various layers that drive them in order to charge ahead, and not only stay alive but thrive.

The Layers of a Bullhearted Brand

A lot of times when professionals discuss "branding," they are myopically focused on the components we're about to cover. As clearly illustrated in preceding chapters, there is much more to developing and fostering a powerful brand than solely focusing on the company itself. But now that we've fully covered the importance and nuances of the Patron and the Positioning, it's time to work on the brand itself, as expressed through the company's multiple layers or platforms.

5. Core Layers of a Brand

From this point forward, we'll use the term "brand" to mean the company itself, rather than the full Golden Lasso representation. A brand is made up of four platforms: Purpose, Personality, Product, and Presentation. In this chapter, we're going to dive into the details of the first three. We'll cover the Presentation layer in Chapter 6.

It's important to fully understand each of the brand's core three platforms because each one influences the following, and they all ladder up to effectively lassoing your brand closer to the desired Patron. As a result, the brand's Purpose is the absolute most important platform to understand, so it only makes sense that we start there as a first step.

With the brand's Purpose clearly identified, one can embark on excavating the personality traits that guide how the brand behaves and how the purpose guides the details of the brand's Product offering. Additionally, the knowledge garnered from the Position and Patron also must influence the details of the brand's platforms. Not doing so can create a disjointment between the brand and its ability to foster the patronage necessary to realize remarkable success.

When brands make exceptions or shoehorn ideas and initiatives into a brand, the perceptions of that brand are inherently negatively impacted. There is no way to brush that aside or smooth it over. If what's being done isn't adding to and bolstering the brand's platforms, it's most certainly deteriorating them.

If you refer back to the Chipotle story covered earlier in this book, you'll quickly understand how a mismatch can be detrimental to brand perceptions. While Chipotle continues to grow its footprint, anyone with a basic ability to deduce what could happen next can see that the people-related issues could cause the brand to fumble or, at worst, topple.

Therefore, it's imperative that as a brand's platforms are considered, formed, and reinforced, every facet of the business is considered and evaluated through that lens. Anywhere there is a mismatch or something that doesn't quite align, it must be set aside to evaluate and reapproach. Embrace the change! It will make for a stronger, effective brand poised for rapid growth and scale.

Purpose: Why Your Brand Exists and Why It Matters

If you have followed the brand strategy world at all in the last few years, chances are you came across Simon Sinek's "Start with Why" TedTalk.[14] And if that sparked something in you, as it did me, then you most likely picked up his book of the same title.[15] Kudos to you if you did, and if you did not, go get it now!

In his talk and book, Mr. Sinek beautifully outlines the power of purpose in today's business landscape. This is not a new theory in the world of strategy, but it is one of the most compelling approaches to describing it in a way that's easily understood and adopted. Prior to his TedTalk, agencies and consultants have used many words to describe a brand's purpose. Alina Wheeler identified it as a Big Idea in her Brand Identity book.[16] While others have

---

[14] Simon Sinek, "Start with Why—How Great Leaders Inspire Action," TEDx Talk, filmed at Puget Sound, 18:01, https://www.youtube.com/watch?v=u4ZoJKF_VuA.

[15] Simon Sinek, *Start with Why: How Great Leaders Inspire Everyone to Take Action* (New York, NY: Penguin, 2009).

[16] Alina Wheeler, *Designing Brand Identity: An Essential Guide for the Whole Branding Team*, 4th ed. (Hoboken, NJ: John Wiley & Sons, 2013).

5. Core Layers of a Brand

called it a brand mantra, "north star," or other metaphor that illustrates the impact and profound importance of a reason for being. Sinek calls it a "why."

All of these names boil down to one word: Purpose. On Merriam-Webster's website,[17] the word Purpose is defined as "something set up as an object or end to be attained: INTENTION." Diving further, the word "Intention" is defined as "what one intends to do or bring about."[18] We add more weight to the word in our own definition by defining it as a reason for being.

Your brand's Purpose must answer the question of "Why?" Why does this brand exist in the purest sense? Why does it matter in this world and to the world of the Patron? Answering this question isn't simple or easy, but answer it you must. Here is a little tip: Your brand's purpose is not about the food you make or the level of service you provide. It's much deeper than that.

A strong Purpose is a guiding light for everything a brand does. It affects the actions and policies of a brand from the top-down, inside-out. It gives reason for what the brand does, the Product, and how it does it, the Personality. It informs messaging and communications from visual and verbal to experiential and digital. In short, the brand's purpose should influence everything and infuse throughout every part of the company.

One of the strongest, most well-known Purpose statements is held

---

[17] Merriam Webster Online, s.v. "purpose," accessed April 14, 2021, https://www.merriam-webster.com/dictionary/purpose.

[18] Merriam Webster Online, s.v. "intention," accessed April 14, 2021, https://www.merriam-webster.com/dictionary/intention.

by the brand Apple. Try not to roll your eyes at this. I fully realize that Apple is used often as an example of success. But in this case, it's a fantastic case to unpack, and it aligns with Sinek's take on brand strategy.

Apple's Purpose is to "think different."[19] Everything they do ladders up to this driving force, and you can see it in everything they do. I always love it when I come across someone who can't wrap their head around Apple's "magic." In their view, they strictly look at the features and benefits of the product in question. Comparing apples to apples, pun intended, they see other products that have a large list of additional benefits beyond those found with Apple products. They see other brands who were first to market with an arguably better product, yet Apple comes in after and dominates.

All of their assessments are true when evaluating with objective facts and reason. Therein lies the problem. Humans are not objective beings. We are driven by emotion, now more than ever. We have so many choices in this world that simple, binary better vs. worse comparisons are way in our past. Instead, we have fantastic options with fantastic features that mostly align. So what is left over for that evaluation? The brand's purpose, how it manifests, and how it can represent their projected values.

Apple is powered by its purpose of thinking different. Everything they do starts with that purpose. It's infused into what they do and how they do it. As a result, purchasing an Apple product injects that value into the suite of brands of the Patron. When a person chooses an Apple product, they feel like their own uniqueness and their

---

[19] Apple, "Apple—Think Different—Full Version," YouTube video, September 30, 2013, https://www.youtube.com/watch?v=5sMBhDv4sik.

desire for design and aesthetics are on full display.

It would be easy to relegate this depth of strategy and thinking as something only useful in the world of technology or other global industries but not the restaurant, beverage, or hospitality industry. That would be absolutely wrong.

Restaurant, beverage, and hospitality industries are three of the most commoditized, competitive in existence today. The competition is fierce, and the positioning of each product in the multiple categories is highly nuanced. There exists a predominance of myopic dependence on features and benefits. But, as you should now know, that's not enough.

With so much competition fighting for share of mind and mouth using only features and benefits, authentic Purpose-driven branding is the only method of getting awareness, interest, and loyalty. When purpose is effectively engaged, fostered, and built, that brand can rapidly rise to the top. It can charge the head of the herd.

But how do you identify a brand's purpose? What tricks and tools can be used to excavate a purpose deeper than the basics of economics? In the next sections, we'll cover some paths to doing just that so that you can land the plane on a purpose that can drive your brand forward.

Finding Your Purpose: Archetypes

Before we jump into Archetypes, it's important to understand that one singular section in a book could never cover the topic fully. To fully immerse in the power of archetypes and how they can be wielded as a tool for brand purpose, view the appendix at the end of this book for some suggested reading options. That said, let's skim the surface on archetypes and how to use archetypes to find a brand's purpose.

Archetypes, like Purpose statements, have many definitions. Initially identified by famous psychologist Carl Jung archetypes have gained traction across that field of study and elsewhere, including branding. Jung's archetypes "are defined as universal, archaic symbols and images that derive from the collective unconscious."[20] Furthermore, an archetype is "the psychic counterpart of instinct. It is described as a kind of innate unspecific [sic] knowledge, derived from the sum total of human history, which prefigures and directs conscious behavior."[21]

Put simply, archetypes are story arcs found across cultures and time periods that psychologically drive human behaviors. And that last part is the most important: they drive human behaviors.

When an archetype is activated throughout a brand, from its purpose through every other area, it influences behaviors in Patrons. The power of archetypes subliminally motivates alignment from the Patron to a brand as they share the same goals in the universe.

This may sound a bit frou-frou and heady, except when one steps back to fully understand why brands engage in branding, marketing, public relations, and everything in between. We're trying to shift behaviors. We want people to buy our food and choose our brand. We want people to say "no" to the brands they already know

---

[20] "Jungian Archetypes," Wikipedia, last modified April 9, 2021, https://en.wikipedia.org/w/index.php?title=Jungian_archetypes&oldid=1016777524.

[21] Ibid.

and love and make our brand their choice. That's a tall order to fill, and the root of the solution is psychological. So, yes, it is cerebral and heady and oftentimes may seem ethereal, but it is very much necessary and profoundly important.

Throughout Jung's work and career, he iterated and further defined archetypes tying them to life stages and events, human behaviors, and even correlating them to energy and lightwaves.[22] He eventually distilled his thinking into twelve core archetypes that serve as the basis for our needs in branding and marketing.[23]

The twelve core archetypes serve as guides for influencing your brand's motivations and goals. They are to be used to identify a reality in the world and Patron, giving context to where the Patron exists in their mental state and where they wish to go. It is that desired shift and that end goal that helps a brand position itself as a tool or guide, for helping reach the results in focus.

A quick example is in the standard understanding of teenagers. While spending their life under the careful watch and guidance of their parental figures, they have been provided a world of safety and stability. That need is fulfilled. But their sense of self and individualism is in short supply and calls to them from their psyche. It drives them to take actions that seek to shed the skin of stability and safety as provided by the family in search of their own self. They look for freedom and fulfillment.

In this example, the anecdotal teenager would align with brands

---

[22] Ibid.

[23] Ibid.

that are driven by the three core archetypes that represent the need for fulfillment: The Explorer, The Sage, and The Innocent. (Checkout *The Hero & The Outlaw* for a full dive into this subject.) In these three archetypes, our teenager finds paths to attaining their freedom. With The Explorer, the path is through adventure and finding new, undiscovered experiences. The Sage promotes a path of finding fulfillment through knowledge, and The Innocent believes that freedom is found in the here and now through faith and righteousness (not necessarily religious.)

All three archetypes offer opportunities for brands to become beacons for that desired state of fulfillment through the archetype's influential means. Whether you've put it together or not, there are well-known brands today that are leveraging the power of these archetypes. Once you know who they are and the archetype they represent, I believe things will click.

Brands that adopt The Explorer archetype promote adventure and exploration. Patagonia, National Geographic, Clif Bar, and American Express are some non-hospitality brands in this archetypal category. In the hospitality category, one could assign brands like Chipotle, Tin Cup Whiskey, and Hotel Indigo as manifesting The Explorer archetype. Each of these brands challenges the Patron to explore, try new things, and search for something new and wonderful. Each of these brands is thriving in its category as a result.

We use archetypes to aid in excavating and identifying a brand's purpose statement. This is accomplished through a series of exercises involving a deck of archetype cards. The best deck I have found to date was compiled by the design studio, Chen Design. In their workbook, *Archetypes in Branding*,[24] they include a simple to follow plan for using archetype cards and the cards themselves.

Their deck includes the twelve core Jungian archetypes with an additional four sub-archetypes for each, totaling sixty archetypes. I have found that the nuances of the twelve core archetypes make for a fantastic series of exercises that lands on one core archetype for the brand to use moving forward.

A brand can only be driven by one archetype. There are arguments countering this statement, but I believe them to be incorrect for a number of reasons. The most important reason is that of the behavioral influence archetypes provide. By choosing multiple archetypes, a brand is essentially gunning for influencing behaviors that cancel each other out. For instance, if a brand identifies The Hero and The Ruler archetypes as the two it aligns with most, the results would be destructive and self-defeating. The Hero is driven by a need for mastery and risk-taking with the means of challenging authority and fighting a system of control. The Ruler is driven by a need for exerting control through stability and structure. They are antithetical to each other and no brand can simultaneously wield the power of both.

The rabbit hole of archetypes runs deep, but this book is only so long, and your attention only so much. My suggestion is to develop a deeper understanding of archetypes through the other resources listed in the appendix so you can leverage their power for your brand's strategy. And powerful they are. When integrated and leveraged effectively, archetypes can effectively influence a brand's

---

[24] Margaret Hartwell and Joshua Chen, *Archetypes in Branding: A Toolkit for Creatives and Strategists* (How Books, 2012).

purpose in a way that will rapidly attract and grow a loyal following.

Finding Your Purpose: Five Whys

Another method of finding your brand's Purpose is to engage in a Five Whys exercise. This technique was originally developed by Sakichi Toyoda. He applied it within the Toyota Motor Corporation while developing the company's manufacturing methodologies. Today, it's a foundational element of Toyota's problem-solving training.[25]

The Toyota Production System's architect, Taiichi Ohno, described the Five Whys method as "the basis of Toyota's scientific approach by repeating why five times the nature of the problem as well as its solution becomes clear."[26] Even though this technique was developed to identify root causes of issues in production, it can be effectively used to excavate a brand's purpose. At the very least, it can help home in on a brand's purpose to clear space for final thinking, while identifying what the brand is clearly not.

Five Whys work so well because it's incredibly simple in theory and practice. One simply asks the question "Why?" five times starting with an initial problem. For Toyota, the system may work as follows starting with the problem of a vehicle not starting.

The vehicle will not start!

---

[25] Taiichi Ohno, "Ask 'Why' Five Times about Every Matter," Toyota, March 2006, https://www.toyota-myanmar.com/about-toyota/toyota-traditions/quality/ask-why-five-times-about-every-matter

[26] "Five Whys," *Wikipedia*, last modified April 5, 2021, https://en.wikipedia.org/w/index.php?title=Five_whys&oldid=1016178581.

5. Core Layers of a Brand

Why? – The battery is dead. (First why)

Why? – The alternator is not functioning. (Second why)

Why? – The alternator belt has broken. (Third why)

Why? – The alternator belt was well beyond its useful service life and not replaced. (Fourth why)

Why? – The vehicle was not maintained according to the recommended service schedule. (Fifth why, a root cause)[27]

It's easy to see how the question of "Why" can easily help drill down to the root cause of a problem, and why asking that question prevents solutions from being developed that fixate on the wrong issue. Without the Five Whys approach, engineers may find themselves fixing the issue of a dead battery or replacing an alternator. While that may fix the problem at first, the root cause still exists, and those problems will manifest again and again until a proper solution is developed and integrated.

You may be thinking: "That's all well and good for engineering problems, but what does that have to do with finding a brand purpose?" Glad you asked.

Employing the Five Whys approach to excavating a brand's purpose isn't a far leap in the slightest. There exists a problem. The problem is not knowing the brand's true purpose, but that's not the starting point. Instead, we start with a statement that's driving the desire to open a restaurant. That's the beginning of the Five Whys where you

---

[27] Steven Spear, *The High Velocity Edge: How Market Leaders Leverage Operational Excellence to Beat the Competition* (New York, NY: McGraw-Hill, 2010), quoted in "Five Whys," Wikipedia.

seek to drill down to the true, core Purpose of your brand.

As stated earlier, your brand's Purpose goes way deeper than the basics of economics. Furthermore, having a passion for a type of food isn't a real Purpose either. I mean, who doesn't love pizza, am I right? A brand's true Purpose is much more profound and usually will not include food at all. Again, Apple's purpose doesn't mention computers, technology, music, or anything of the sort. It's to Think Different.

Here's an example of how the Five Whys technique can work for a restaurant brand:

I want to open a burrito restaurant brand.

Why? – Because I love burritos and creating new burrito flavors. (First why)

Why? – It's something I'm good at, and I love the flavor. (Second why)

Why? – It reminds me of my family and growing up. (Third why)

Why? – Because we used to cook together, and they taught me how to make burritos. (Fourth why)

Why? – It's an easy-to-make, inexpensive food. (Fifth why)

In this example, the Purpose driving this vision ahead would be something relating to the convenience and cost-effectiveness of the burrito. With a little bit of creativity and brainstorming, one may land on the purpose: *To make my family's food and flavors accessible and convenient so no one goes hungry.* From this purpose, and the

Five Whys journey to get to it, comes a number of ideas that can ladder up to that purpose. We'll tap into them in more detail when we unpack the Personality and Product layers.

Despite its simplicity, it can be difficult to do alone as it requires a highly objective guide that is not afraid to push and prod for better responses from the person answering the questions. Oftentimes, having an unbiased person to challenge your thinking can help identify a true purpose. Without that objectivity, one may land with a purpose that's untrue and inauthentic. Sometimes shoehorning a Purpose statement into an existing vision is the easier approach, but doing so will be akin to building a house on sand. And we all know how that proverb ends.

Personality: The Unique Attitude That Sets You Apart

Personality is what gives a brand nuance and attitude, and that's why it exists as the layer just outside the Purpose. A brand's personality traits define its "how." They guide how the brand acts and behaves from internal to external and verbal through visual. No wonder it's one of the core layers that must be well defined for any brand strategy to effectively come to life.

A brand's personality traits empower all parties to bring the brand to life with a clear path. Rather than starting from square one with a blank canvas, the brand's personality helps identify some potential paths forward. Think of it as staring at a huge closet of clothing and shoes. In this closet is a wide selection of clothing from the ultra-formal tuxedo and accompanying cumberbund to torn-up jeans and a raggedy rock t-shirt. The options are seemingly endless. So how do you choose what's the right outfit to wear?

Occasion is the driver of how we select the clothing to wear. If it's an evening wedding reception, we know that black tie is the right fit, so we forgo the rock t-shirt and jeans. If it's a chill night around a firepit with some beers, those jeans and that shirt are the right choices.

When we develop brand experiences, we set the occasion through our personality layer. If our personality is rustic, heritage, and earthy, then designing an identity that's vibrant, urban, and offbeat is not going to jive well at all. Answering the restaurant's phone with "Hello my fine sir, thank you for telephoning the illustrious house of fine flavors" will seem completely odd. The personality helps us align all components of a brand to ensure they ladder up to a cohesive, believable experience.

Believability is the name of the game. Have you ever met a person who claimed to be one thing, but acted and presented themselves counterintuitively to that claim? It's off-putting and uncomfortable. It immediately instills a sense of distrust in the individual. Once trust and believability are lost, they're hard to regain.

A believable brand personality is only as good as how unique it is when compared to competing brands. Brands must have a personality that helps reinforce their position in the market. This is all about getting attention and establishing your brand as different. So falling in line with what others do is a bad move. Remember, positioning is critical to success.

When it comes to personality traits, I've found that many leaders tend to go with some common descriptors. If I had a dollar for every time a leader emphatically exclaimed that their brand is truly "fun," I'd have a ton of cash. (Realistically I'd probably have a thousand dollars, but "a ton" sounds better.) These common descriptors can fool one into thinking they're truly different when, in fact, they aren't. After all, what brand doesn't want to be "fun?"

It's important to dig deep into unique adjectives that tap bits of the brand's personality that are ownable. To that end, it's equally important to know of some adjectives that have been overused and, as a result, have lost their meaning and merit. Here are a few cliché adjectives that come to mind:

Craft/Artisan. Everyone thinks they have craft food and cocktails, and everyone likes to state it over and over again. This is not unique, and it gets ignored.

Farm-to-BLANK. The "Farm-to" movement is way past being on-trend. At this point, a lot of the sourcing stories are expected and not a differentiator. It's important to give nuance to why this approach matters to the Patron, rather than blurting it out every chance you get.

Fun. Yeah, we know. Every place wants to be fun. Just like "being cool," being fun is not something you say, it's something you simply are. Saying it reduces or removes credibility.

Good Service. You're in the service industry, so this would be table stakes. Define what makes "good service" from your brand instead of simply stating it'll be "good."

Approachable. I can't think of any restaurant brand that has specifically wanted to be unapproachable making this another ineffective adjective.

Reinventing. I laugh every time I come across a statement of "reinventing _____." Mainly because rarely is the concept reinventing anything. It's a bloated, pompous statement and adjective that should be avoided.

Green. Being earth-friendly and lowering a carbon footprint is part of a bigger Purpose and effort. It should not be a brand personality trait. If being green is important to you and your company, then it should be woven throughout every aspect of the business and not used simply as a personality trait.

Authentic. While this can be true and can be done, it is a forever commitment to never doing anything inauthentic. Therefore, it's a big undertaking that essentially challenges Patrons to be hypersensitive to the level of authenticity delivered. Our suggestion is to steer clear unless you're fully bought in and committed to never doing anything that can be perceived as inauthentic.

Identifying your brand's unique attributes is a critically important exercise. Once established, these three traits will affect every aspect of the brand empowering you and your teams with the knowledge to identify what builds the brand and what does not. Strong, unique personality traits ensure the brand can effectively grab attention while reinforcing a clear position against competitors. My advice is to push to identify the traits your brand, and only your brand, can truly own. Let's dive into how to start that process.

How to Identify Your Brand's Personality Traits

Identifying a brand's personality traits may seem like an easy task. As humans, we spend our existence defining the world around us, so how hard can selecting a few adjectives about a brand be? Actually, quite hard indeed.

It's not as simple as throwing some adjectives together and calling it day. A brand's personality is so crucial that doing so would be negligent and dangerous to realizing success and growth. What compounds the issue is the difficulty of narrowing down the list of adjectives to describe a brand. It can be bright, fun, upbeat, loud, eccentric, quirky, goofy, and bubbly all at the same time. Having eight personality traits is difficult to manage, activate, and evaluate.

I have found that distilling a brand's personality into three cumulative and overlapping personality traits creates the strongest foundations. With the power of three, one can easily manage the nuances of the tone of voice and visuals. It becomes easier to activate the brand across channels and certainly easier to evaluate the ongoing development of the brand once it's launched into the world.

With three being the magic number, one can embark on excavating and identifying a brand's personality. At Vigor, we have found that word listing is the best tool for the job. It's easy to do and requires very few tools. It's also quite fun, or at least I think so. #BrandNerd

Before diving into the word listing exercise, it's important to mention that more brains are better than one. This isn't an exercise you should do alone. But having people who don't understand the brand is also a bad move. You should choose 3-5 individuals who understand the brand's Patron, Position, and Purpose, as well as the vision of the leader. They should feel comfortable challenging others in a constructive way and have a profound ability to deductively think through details of strategy.

In the corporate world this is much easier than in the startup phase, but the need for multiple points of view remains the same. What people create together is often better than what each can do alone because, together, they are more than the sum of their parts. A brand can realize its true personality traits and the details that make them uniquely attributable to the brand itself.

Once you have your group identified, get them in a room, and be sure to supply refreshments. Start with a writing implement and a surface. This should be a whiteboard and dry-erase marker, but if you've chosen to go it alone, a pen and paper or even a computer and blank document will work just as well.

On the whiteboard, write the brand's Patron name, its Positioning statement, and its Purpose for easy reference. From there, start writing every single word—adjective, verb, or noun—that comes to mind when thinking of the brand. Pull no punches, no holds barred. Now is not the time for editing. Even duplicates are allowed. In fact, duplicates can be a way of identifying a word that has consensus. Do this until you've exhausted everyone's brain, then put your marker down and take a break for an hour, a few hours, or a day.

The break is extremely important. It allows your brain to reset while ruminating over the brand's personality. When you return, you'll be surprised as to how many more words you can think of after you've given your brain that reset time.

When you've finally hit the bottom of the barrel of ideas, it's time to start editing. To edit effectively, you'll need to keep in mind the brand's competitive set and the words they use to describe their concept. It's important you do not inadvertently land on a descriptive word that's shared with a competitor. Remember, we're looking to differentiate!

Your goal is to edit the word list down to ten words. These ten words should describe nuances of the brand. They will become words to use for the brand's verbal identity: the writing and speech-related part of your brand's Presentation layer. But wait, there's more.

From that list of ten, the final step is to drill down into a combination of three words total that collectively describe the brand at its core. These three traits will be used to evaluate every single part of the brand's Product and Presentation layers, so they better be 100% accurate.

Your brand's three traits don't exist as individual components. They work together, in unison at all times. For instance, Vigor's personality traits are Courageous, Empathetic, and Principled. We are not solely Courageous or Empathetic alone. Everything we do seeks to be the combination of the three, creating a fully on-brand experience and manifestation of our personality.

The final step is to give each of the three traits a little more flavor. Weave the original ten descriptive words into short narrative descriptions for each trait. This adds nuance and deeper understanding to what is meant by each word and how they relate to one another.

Gandhi and Che: Wildly Different, Oddly Similar

If you're familiar with these two historical figures and what they did in their lifetimes, it's okay to be scratching your head right now. Upon first glance, no two individuals could be more wildly different. Mahatma Gandhi, a symbol of peace and harmony, somehow is being compared to Ernesto Rafael "Che" Guevara de la Serna, a Marxist revolutionary and guerilla leader in Cuba. For those unfamiliar, let's dig into each figure just so there's a level understanding.

Mahatma Gandhi, according to Wikipedia, was " an Indian lawyer, anti-colonial nationalist, and political ethicist, who employed nonviolent resistance to lead the successful campaign for India's independence from British rule, and in turn, inspired movements for civil rights and freedom across the world."[28] Through peaceful, benevolent means, Gandhi showed the world that revolution can happen without violence and war.

Photograph by Rühe, Public Domain

---

[28] "Mahatma Gandi," *Wikipedia*, last modified April 14, 2021, https://en.wikipedia.org/w/index.php?title=Mahatma_Gandhi&oldid=1017756052

Ernesto Rafael "Che" Guevara de la Serna, according to Wikipedia, was "was an Argentine nationalized Cuban, Marxist revolutionary, guerrilla leader, physician, author, diplomat, and military theorist. A major figure of the Cuban Revolution."[29] Beyond becoming a popular graphic for t-shirts adorned by would-be rebellious youth, Che was a highly violent enforcer for Fidel Castro. He oversaw and carried out the murder of countless political dissenters to clear the path for a Socialist regime that would threaten liberty and freedom-led countries, including the United States.

Photograph by Alberto Korda, public domain

How, in God's name, are these two figures anything alike? They are both rebels, and their stories are rooted in the Outlaw archetype.

Despite their wildly different means of achieving revolution, these two individuals sought to affect change in their worlds. That is the root behavioral driver behind the Outlaw archetype and the other two archetypes that share that quadrant (The Hero and The Magician.) The Outlaw seeks to shift power structures and perceived injustices through any means necessary, even if that means breaking the law. Both Gandhi and Che did just that but in their own ways. And that's the basis for the relationship between a brand's archetypal driver and its Personality layer.

---

[29] "Che Guevara," *Wikipedia*, last modified April 11, 2021, https://en.wikipedia.org/w/index.php?title=Che_Guevara&oldid=1017264031.

It's alluring to make presumptions of a brand's would-be personality based on its archetype. A Sage archetype brings forth imagery of Yoda, Morpheus from the *Matrix* trilogy, and otherwise sherpas. The attitudes are stoic and sometimes austere. From this imagery, presumptuous attitudes of brainy, cold, direct, and objective can emerge. That's a mistake.

A brand's archetypal driver and its personality are two different layers of the bigger picture. The archetype is a behavioral driver that affects the brand's Purpose. It answers Why the brand exists. The Personality is the method and style in which that Purpose is achieved. It answers How the brand does what it does.

Che was driven by an Outlaw archetype through the Personality of intolerance, aggressiveness, and charisma. Gandhi through the Personality of peacefulness, harmony, and benevolence. Both achieved their goals, both in their own ways.

The lesson here is to let your brand's archetype drive behavior and give direction to your brand's purpose, while allowing the Personality free-rein to dictate the attitude and vibe of how the Purpose is sought after and achieved.

Product: What the Brand Brings to the World

Finally, we're at the part where we talk about "good product and good service." Note: when it comes to developing the brand, "service" is also the product. See? I told you it had a role in branding! A brand's Product layer is a combination of its menu offering, service model, and philanthropic endeavors. It delivers the

"What" of the brand, serving as a means to work towards achieving the brand's Purpose.

This is where operations and culinary leadership need to collaborate heavily. It's why ensuring they are part of the process from day one is vitally important to brand success. Your culinary and operations leaders need to understand and agree with the brand's strategy fully in order to interpret it into their respective disciplines and areas of responsibility.

It's the responsibility of the leader to ensure that these leaders are at the table and that they understand why they are there and what's expected of them from the very beginning. Leaders must encourage collaboration and open-mindedness with the process to ensure ops and culinary aren't simply doing as they're told but, instead, feel energized and empowered to push the brand's offering beyond the status quo.

Food & Beverage

A restaurant's product is usually the first thing that comes into clarity. More often than not, it's the entire reason the restaurant has even been dreamt up. The restaurant's culinary offering is usually born of passion for the cuisine or strokes of genius. Countless restaurants have been opened with the food and service being the sole driving force behind the brand. Some have succeeded. Many have not.

The Product layer must be driven by the other layers of the brand's strategy: the Purpose and Personality. Using them as a lens, the core cuisine should be reimagined and shifted to create a unique offering that not only supports the brand but also bolsters it and makes it stronger. Misalignment or failure to reconsider a product offering through the brand lens creates a gap in the overall experience. As you should know by now, gaps are bad. They are openings for disbelief and distrust, slowly rotting away chances of future success.

To demonstrate the right way to refine a brand's Product layer through the Purpose and Personality, I will use a former client of ours, SlapFish. When SlapFish came to Vigor, they had great foundations of their brand already in place. The food was awesome, the service was great, and the experience was fresh overall. But things weren't 100% lined up and the brand felt disjointed. It was missing a well-defined purpose.

Through our collaborative strategic workshops and efforts, we were able to excavate a true passion sourced from the heart of SlapFish's founder. The brand's purpose was to "make seafood matter." In the seafood landscape, there exists a lot of disinformation and abuse of the word "sustainable."

Major suppliers throw it around in their collateral and presentations to sell their seafood product to restaurants. And a lot of places buy-in then adopt the abuse of the word for marketing purposes. One can find this word across the websites of brands like Red Lobster and Captain D's. Red Lobster even has a video intending to send home the belief in sustainability.[30] You can imagine what it includes: A fisherman on a boat on the ocean talking about the process of catching the fish and lobsters. It feels genuine, but anyone with a bit of critical thinking has to be skeptical of their claims.

---

[30] "Red Lobster—'Sustainability,'—Longform" Vimeo.com, accessed April 14, 2021, https://vimeo.com/161822847

The fact is, much of the oceanic seafood eaten in the United States is flash-frozen at sea. They use chemicals to preserve the seafood to ensure it stays "fresh." SlapFish's question to the world: "Is spraying food with ammonia-based chemicals truly sustainable? Is it even something we should be eating?" Their stance is a very loud, irreverent "No!"

Through our work, we uncovered SlapFish's personality traits. The brand was poised to truly own the attitude mixing maverick, unreserved, and expressiveness. It's these traits that were used as a lens to evaluate the brand's Product and Presentation layers.

Together, we ideated on increasing the amount of perceived expertise and passion for sustainable seafood in a way that was uninhibited from being loud and ruffling some feathers. When evaluating the food offering, we uncovered opportunities to introduce reasons to believe the brand's claims from local catch items and off the wall takes on classic dishes. We leaped from the brand's most interesting item, Chowder Fries and encouraged them to find new ways to be unreserved in their culinary and beverage thinking. Why? Because with every element that uplifts and represents a brand's attitude, that attitude becomes more believable. Believability is the root of trust.

Service

The service model and day parts are the other components of a brand's Product layer. They are equally as important to the perceptions of the brand and can be tailored to the brand's unique personality. The service model is the method in which the food is provided, and the brand should have a say in that.

The brand's Purpose and Personality help make clear what service model makes the most sense and what that service sounds like. For instance, when someone calls the restaurant, does the person who picks up the phone say, "Howdy y'all?" or do they say, "Thank you for calling Blank Restaurant, how may I help you?" Both are friendly enough and provide arguably good service, but both are quite different, and they correlate to developing a perception of the restaurant and its experience.

If the brand is vying for an elevated approach to food with the intent of pushing the boundaries of worldly cuisine, a drive-through quick-serve format wouldn't make much sense. It'd be like a snooty trust fund kid without a financial care in the world trying to relate to a heavy metal drummer living hand to mouth. Sorry kid, that doesn't fly.

Misalignment in experience can be felt on a visceral level at times. Have you ever had a waiter in a fancy restaurant who was way too lax and familiar? It just doesn't feel right. It makes the experience feel less valuable and misaligned. Even if you're not cognizant of what's happening, you walk away feeling as if you were delivered a less than ideal experience. Cue the negative Yelp reviews.

Once a brand strategy has its archetypal driver, Purpose, and Personality in place, each of the leaders should be encouraged to revisit their original ideas of food and service through that lens. They should be asked to come back to the table with adjustments to the operations from culinary through procedures and even down to operating supplies. Using the brand's Personality they should be able to shift the elements under their control and influence into a more unified experience.

Philanthropy

The final component of a brand's Product layer is what it does for the community. And this one is very difficult because most people have a big heart and want to do whatever they can to help others in need. But you cannot be everything to everyone, and that rings true in the philanthropic space as well.

It may sound counterintuitive to the tenets of charity, but what you do for the world should align with your brand's purpose. It's not that donating money to the local Elks club won't do something good. The question is more in the realm of could your charity and your efforts have done much more? The answer is, yes.

When a brand identifies an organization or effort that aligns with its own Purpose, that brand creates a powerful partnership that gets way more traction. Patrons can make the connection with the brand and that philanthropic effort quickly and develop belief in the altruistic nature of the partnership.

Far too often, brands get aligned with charities that pose a very clear mismatch. When this happens the efforts to raise money and awareness don't reach the full potential that could be found with stronger initiatives. At the very worst, the effort seems like a ploy to increase sales and traffic, rather than an honest effort to make the world a better place.

An effective alignment of brand strategy and philanthropy can be found with our friends at Johnny's Pizza House. Johnny's is a regional pizza staple found in Louisiana. Started by Johnny Huntsman in 1973, his namesake Pizza House grew into a dominant brand putting up a respectable fight against the "big guys." In recent years, the brand launched efforts to raise money for Susan G. Komen by adding pink sprinkles to the tops of their cinnamon sticks. Sales of this product went towards a donation to the well-known breast cancer research organization.

You may be shrugging your shoulders in a "so what?" manner, and that's fair. After all, who's complaining that the brand is raising money for Susan G. Komen? Is there really a problem with that? Not really, but as I stated earlier, the question is could their efforts do even more good with a better-aligned recipient?

We definitely thought the answer was, "yes." Together with Johnny's, we sought to find a nonprofit that would better align with the brand's dedication to their local communities. Johnny's had already been known to give well into the six figures to local sports, academics, and religious organizations. But it's hard to tap into that grouping in a way that's easy to remember. We worked together to try to identify a larger fund that would help make a stronger impact with the donated dollars. Nothing really seemed to align.

Then tragedy struck the company. Mr. Huntsman had lost his battle with Alzheimer's. However, in the aftermath, the answer to the question became quite clear. Johnny's Pizza House was best suited to help a disease that affects way too many households across the world and in their community. It was a pure alignment of the brand's dedication to the community, and it was true to the heart of the brand.

The year following the tragic loss of Johnny, his pizza house brand launched purple sprinkles on their cinnamon sticks to raise money for Alzheimer's research. Throughout the year they've started participating in walks to raise even more money and have full buy-in from the team and community.

When a brand identifies a philanthropic effort that aligns with its own strategy, the Patrons take notice. They're quicker to buy-in and trust that the motives are pure, resulting in success across the board. The brand gets notoriety and builds awareness. The charity sees more benefits that last longer. It's truly a win-win, and it's derived from understanding the components of the brand's strategic layers.

In Real Life: How a Brand Misalignment Created a not so Yummy QSR Failure

Serial restaurateurs are in a never-ending search for the next big thing. We encounter a lot of these folks in our day-to-day operations. Our ability to reflect their excitement and find a path to success positions us as a fantastic partner–if only they listen. Sometimes they strike gold, but many other times they miss the mark only to start all over again. It's like a fly to a zapping light. They just cannot help it.

In 2011, we connected with a gentleman who was hyped up on bao buns. In case you don't know, bao buns are an Asian bread-like dumpling shaped in a ball and filled with different savory fillings. Chicken curry and red bean paste are two of the most popular. However, why stop there? That's exactly what Mark (name changed to protect the innocent) thought.

Mark began to develop a menu centered on the bao buns. It wasn't so crazy because there were a number of concepts already surging ahead with that product as the hero. Wow Bao was one of the top players. With that proof of concept, he launched into finding a bao bun machine that could mass-produce the product while simultaneously developing the first location.

When Mark connected with us, he had already decided on a name, tagline, and logo. We were to jump in and help get it across the finish line with the other touchpoints that would mount to a fully fleshed-out visual identity. Normally we shy away from this type of scenario, but we believed in the concept and we believed in Mark, at first.

Before jumping in, we did an assessment of the identity from name through logo. With fresh eyes, it's usually easy to see some red flags, and we were seeing many. First off, the name. Mark had fallen in love with the name YumBunz, and he had given extra flavor to it with the description "Dim Sum Fast." Despite the extra descriptive power, that line only added to the confusion.

We lightly tested the name and the description with a small group of locals who were representative of the brand's desired Patron. Every single one of them was confused by the name, mistaking it for a bakery. The description only compounded the confusion. You see, "dim sum" comes with a lot of preconceived notions. People imagine a small cart full of tapas-like small plates from which you can pull. YumBunz offered none of that. In fact, the only dim sum standard you would find on the menu was the bao buns.

Maybe the confusion would be cleared up by the logo, we thought. Nope. The logo further muddied the waters and left the test group participants scratching their heads. To make matters worse, the logo looked cheap and sterile with very little unique character. We discussed our plan of action and decided to bring the findings to Mark and suggest that we engage in a full brand strategy process to help get the foundations in the right place.

Being the zealous restaurateur he was, Mark responded with a smirk and shrugged it all off. He fervently declined the brand strategy suggestion and wouldn't entertain a change of name, slogan, or logo. In his words, he knew it would work as-is, and he didn't have the time to change it because a few people didn't get it. He demanded we move forward as is.

After pleading our case one more time to no avail, we proceeded ahead to do our best to help overcome the barriers created by a bad name and logo. We started making some headway when we came across some fresh press about the concept. In this press, Mark was touting the hand-made buns, and how they'll be fresh-made in the kitchen and served hot. He went on to discuss the "dim sum fast" slogan and what it meant, alluding to an extended menu that featured zero dim sum staples. I was genuinely confused so I called up Mark and planned to meet.

He greeted me at the door with his wide smile. "You saw the press, right? How great was it? That should get people really excited about what we're doing," he exclaimed. I responded with my concerns and confusion. I asked if he'd changed the menu and scrapped the machine in the warehouse. He laughed and said, "of course not, but who will know and who cares?"

That line rang in my ears like a siren wailing in warning. I left that meeting disheartened and annoyed. This guy had the basis of a great concept, but he refused to heed any precautions, listen to any feedback, and now he was pleased to be lying to the public. I knew we had to disengage as fast as possible, so when I returned to the office I wrote the email informing him of the decision and accompanied it with a link to all the assets created up to that moment. He replied with, "thanks."

YumBunz opened with much acclaim and lines out of the door. People were super excited about the concept. Reviews began popping up about how good the food was, but how it was dim sum, and they didn't really understand the name. They also complained about wait times and the kitchen running out of food. There are worse things to have happened, and they did just open, so everyone seemed to give them a pass. But then the inevitable happened. Someone leaked that the bao were not made in-house at all. They were made in a factory.

The breaking of that story sunk YumBuz in a matter of weeks. Mark scrambled to shift the concept, chalking the failure up to people "not getting it." Despite shifting to a Vietnamese offering including pho, the damage had already been done and YumBunz closed six weeks after opening.

In every story of massive failure, there are pivotal moments where a different choice could've had a different end. It'd be speculation to say that had Mark listened, YumBunz would have succeeded. But who's to know if that's the truth. What I do know to be true is that when people say they don't get something or that something is confusing, it's probably not a good idea to move forward. Furthermore, when you lie to the public, it's only a matter of time before they find out and reject you outright.

6. Presentation

Bull Story: Sacred Cows

The Story

The sacred cow is an idiom, a figurative reference to sacred cows in some religions. According to Wikipedia, "this idiom is thought to have originated in American English, although similar or even identical idioms occur in many other languages."[31]

"The idiom is based on the popular understanding of the elevated place of cows in Hinduism and appears to have emerged in America in the late 19th century. The reverence for cows in the traditionally agrarian Vedic Hindu society stems from the reluctance to harm an animal whose milk humans consume after being weaned off the mother's milk."[32] In Jewish tradition, there is a similar moral stigma against cooking veal (calf meat) in cows' milk."[33]

Perhaps the most famous sacred cow is found in the Judeo-Christian Bible. In the Old Testament, specifically Exodus 32. For

---

[31] "Sacred Cow (Idiom)," Wikipedia, modified March 17, 2021, https://en.wikipedia.org/w/index.php?title=Sacred_cow_(idiom)&oldid=1012661793.

[32] Ibid.

[33] Ibid.

those unfamiliar with the story, here's the gist:

Moses was called to the top of a mountain to receive laws by which man must abide. These ten laws, or commandments, were scrawled onto stone tablets to be presented to the people. Moses brought the tablets back down to the people only to find them worshipping a golden calf. In his rage, Moses destroyed the tablets containing the commandments in a rage of indignation.

The Lesson: Identities Should Be Profound Expressions

A literal sacred cow or sacred bull is an actual cow or bull that is treated with sincere respect. A figurative sacred cow is a figure of speech for something considered immune from question or criticism. Both cows are present throughout the inner workings of brands. One kind is good, the other is bad.

Let's start with the bad sacred cow, which happens to be the most prevalent. Figurative sacred cows prevent brands from growth across the board. Oftentimes, they serve as seemingly trusted truisms that guide a company to a certain level of success. In the process, their level of sanctity increases creating the perception of a powerful ally. But they are, inevitably, false idols.

At Vigor, we had a client that was desperately looking to pull out of a tailspin. The entire brand had been built in the 90s and early 2000s in locations that guaranteed traffic: mall food courts. Over the years, however,the viability of mall food courts decreased, while rents continued to skyrocket. Leap to 2017 and mall food courts are thriving with consumers who have very little expendable income. They're wrought with extremely unhealthy food offerings, but they can deliver tasty sustenance at a tasty price. In short, cheap food at a cheap price.

This was a trend that was in full opposition to the brand's current offering of salads, wraps, and other items with a halo of healthy perceptions. So, over the years the brand added in items they thought would help fill in the blanks in sales and revenue. Salads were nearly 100% removed, wraps were given cheeses and creamy sauces to "fatten things up." And the menu's prices and perceptions tumbled.

The scenario was and remains in full effect even today. Yet, when we attempted to evolve the brand and propel it forward, we were met with one sacred cow after another. "We HAVE to have wings on the menu; we cannot remove them or we'll fail!" exclaimed a leader in one of our meetings. "Healthy and higher quality food won't sell. It'll make it too expensive," exclaimed another. The team vehemently declined any opportunity to foray outside of food courts despite statistics and data showing this to be the best move for the brand.

Suffice to say, we were at an impasse. And then it struck the team that the path forward may exist in attempting to change their mind, and success could be found in changing the brand itself. Surprisingly enough, we got buy-in and got to work at crafting the strategy, name, identity, and kiosk design. When we got to the name, we hit another sacred cow: complete aversion to any name and a demand to use a retired brand name from decades past.

The new concept opened to the public. Despite the use of the blasé name, it experienced a measurable lift in sales despite. It was the only location opened under the new brand, as the organization turned its sights back to what it knew and what it believed worked. #TheDevilYouKnow

In this case, sacred cows are the death of a company. Leadership is so fatigued it refuses to challenge their perceptions of truth with a "break the china" mentality. As a result, they exist on borrowed time. Despite this bleak scenario, there is another side to the "sacred cow" idiom.

In a lot of ways, your brand's verbal and visual identity, the components of the Presentation layer, must be crafted like a literal sacred cow. A brand's Presentation layer should be a profound expression of everything covered thus far in the book. Much like sacred cows throughout the Hindu faith are adorned with colors, bells, whistles, and over-the-top, gorgeous decor, a brand's presentation should be exalted.

The "sanctity" of a brand identity is found in the correlation between that layer and the reasons to believe the claims as found throughout the strategy. The identity should tie to all the components of the brand, and when that's done well, you have an amazingly unforgettable identity that demands attention. You have something truly sacred.

Presenting The Presentation Layer

We have reached the part where we dive into the brand's Presentation layer (figure 04). The Presentation layer consists of every touchpoint that works to communicate the brand's offering to the Patron in a way that's evocative of the brand's Purpose and Personality. This is where the visual and verbal elements of the brand come to life, and it is usually the part of branding that many

fig. 04

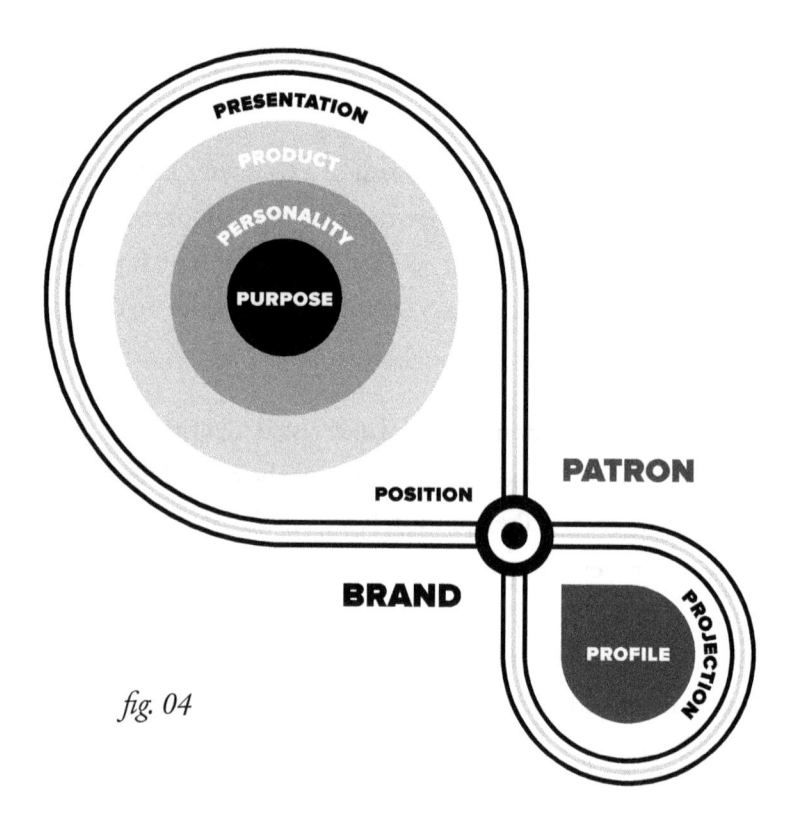

misconceive as the entire meaning of "branding."

Take stock. We're a little over halfway through this book and only now getting to the subject of visual and verbal identity. There's a reason for this, and I hope that by now you understand. The brand is so much more than the things one can touch, hear, see, smell, and taste. And we have spent time covering each of those components in great detail. So, at this point, we have the platforms of the brand in clear view through which we can guide and evaluate this critical layer.

A brand's Presentation layer is informed by its archetype, Purpose, Personality, and Product, but no one element can tell that whole story. One cannot expect a logo to communicate the nuances and intricacies of each of those layers in enough detail for it to sink in. Additionally, no one human can, nor wants to, absorb that amount of information in one moment.

Instead, we must leverage all of the available communication opportunities in the suite of brand touchpoints. That spans the physical and digital spaces. We must craft each moment as an opportunity to unfurl the brand's broader narrative in a way that's fully unique and distinctive to the brand effectively positioning it against the competition. When this is done well, it's profound. The experiences get remembered, and people flock to the restaurant, or should I say the stampede to it?

In this chapter, we'll dive into the components that make up a brand's Presentation layer, while laying down the basics of how to evaluate good design versus bad. That said, the realm of naming and design is vast and ever-growing. Many have dedicated their lives to the multiple disciplines covered under the Presentation layer, and they are constantly learning and growing.

I write all of this to ensure that you understand that we do not have the capacity in one book to cover this topic in great detail. But we will cover the foundational parts to help spark your journey and equip you with enough knowledge to find good partners and identify great design.

Everything Matters. Every. Single. Thing. Matters.

Uniting a brand sets a strong foundation for growth and success. However, in order to thrive, the brand must be propelled forward with a remarkable visual and verbal identity. Successful brands leverage a mix of internal and external communications, marketing, and advertising endeavors communicated visually and verbally through a language of color, typography, photography, copy, sound, tactility, physical space, and digital. Literally, everything that creates a brand experience. And every single thing matters when crafting a brand identity.

Restaurants have no issue forking out hundreds of thousands to millions of dollars in capital to build out locations. The expense is easily justified, and I'm not arguing that investment. After all, the four-wall experience is the culmination of the brand. It should be a gold standard immersion point that fuels functionality and form in ways that are remarkable.

However, when it comes to everything else, restaurants fail to invest the appropriate amount of capital. Logos are thrown together by "graphics people," while names are usually an output of some banter and brainstorms between a few people paying little attention to a brand's strategy. Naming usually rests on the whims and internal vision of a few people, if not one person. One can find this quite easily by asking someone at the restaurant why it has the name it has. The responses will be everything from "I don't know" to "Our chef Kevin likes that flower." This is a horrible way to create a brand that is intended to scale.

If you want to launch, or evolve, a brand that's poised for rapid growth, you must invest in every element of the puzzle. Cut no corners and do things right the first time. That means considering, crafting, and curating every facet of what is seen, heard, and experienced with the brand strategy as a lens.

I'm certain that in your mind you are already thinking of areas where this isn't true or where you think I'm exaggerating. It's okay, I harbor no ill will. I have encountered it often. The most prevalent places where we get budget skepticism and a perception of low importance are in menus and websites. Some chefs feel like their food and plating are so amazing that a piece of paper with centered text is all that's needed for their menu. Some restaurateurs feel a website should cost a couple of thousand US dollars and nothing more.

While they may get away with it to a certain point, those who choose to treat every touchpoint with a level of importance beyond utility go much further because everything matters. Even the type of paper and the style of typography matter. They can help guide perceptions or, if not considered important, they can detract from the desired experience, making an upscale experience feel low-quality or an approachable concept feel too high-end to where it alienates desired Patrons.

Sarah Hyndman has been conducting research on the effects of typography on human perceptions for quite some time now. She's published multiple books on the subject, as well as research papers. Her findings are fantastic. Through Ms. Hyndman's research, she's proven, unequivocally, that typography can guide human perceptions of a brand experience.[34]

Research and studies have shown that tactility affects our perceptions of a brand and food. In a research paper published in the Journal of Consumer Research, Aradhna Krishna and Maureen Morrin conducted a series of experiments involving the perceptual

---

[34] See Sarah Hyndman, Why Fonts Matter (Berkeley, CA: Gingko Press, 2016); Sarah Hyndman, "Type Tasting Books," Type Tasting, accessed April 15, 2021, https://www.typetasting.com/books.

drivers of touch and haptic senses. They found that many people do indeed judge a drink by its container. Specifically, the firmness of a cup seems to have an impact on consumer evaluations of the beverage contained inside.[35]

Their findings transfer across every surface of a physical experience. The material of a counter or table, the materials used for handheld menus, and the other elements with which we engage all ladder up to affect our perceptions of the brand's food and flavor. That means a cheaply produced menu with a layout using certain typography could absolutely destroy the desired perceptions of a brand even if the food and service are stellar. The result would be the feeling of having paid too much for a meal or deterring potential patrons from choosing a restaurant because it doesn't speak to them and their needstate.

Developing a strong, successful brand requires attention to every detail that comprises that brand experience. Therefore, every part of the brand is an important component of crafting the desired perceptions and attracting the desired Patron. Nonchalance, indifference, or outright disbelief in the power of sense beyond taste is negligent and a recipe for failure.

Naming is Hard and That's Okay

Naming should be simple, right? We've all done it at one point or another, whether it's a nickname, a pet, or that first car that you loved to hate. You may even think you have a natural knack for

---

[35] Aradhna Krishna and Maureen Morrin, "Does Touch Affect Taste? The Perceptual Transfer of Product Container Haptic Cues," Journal of Consumer Research 34, no. 6 (2008): 807-818, https://doi.org/10.1086/523286.

it. However, creating a name for a brand isn't as easy as throwing some words or phrases around until something sounds right. In fact, if something "sounds right" it's probably because it's similar to what already exists. Although it may feel good, that feeling masks a dangerous truth: a forgettable name.

Naming has to be one of the most difficult parts of creating a brand and/or product offering. As humans, we encounter countless names, from proper to brands, on a daily basis. We engage in naming throughout our lives, whether it's naming the kids, pets, or a car. The combination of the two makes for a situation where everyone feels they are capable of creating a name for a company and brand. As with most things, it's not that simple.

Yes, anyone can think of a name, but that's not the question. The question is, can anyone think of a name that's unique in the market, ties to the brand's platforms, and is legally ownable? With each of the items in that list, the amount of people who can develop a name becomes very small indeed.

Naming is not an exercise in unencumbered creativity. It's a mix of psychology, linguistics, research, trends, and law. And, it is very much not easy at all. Sometimes, one gets hit with a bolt of lightning-like inspiration, and while awesome, it's not something to bank on. Instead, a process should be applied to developing a name to ensure you don't end up with a figurative sacred cow that creates a weakness in the foundations of the brand.

Have you ever seen a youth soccer game? I'm not talking about middle school or high school. I'm talking about young adolescents playing the game. The ball gets kicked to one area, and everyone on the field charges that area. There's no discipline. There exists no knowledge of the nuances of the game and how to structure attacks. It's wild.

Naming, and even design, is a lot like that game, and one can see it in the trends that ebb and flow. One or two brands find notoriety and fame with a certain naming convention, and a mass of other restaurateurs and brands follow suit without regard for viability or relevance.

Take, for example, the most recent naming trend: the Blank & Blank. While I'm not certain who started the trend, it's safe to say at this point that it's completely played out. The Blank & Blank naming trend hit hard in the mid-2010s and unfortunately is still leveraged today, but not as frequently. These names were defined by obscure nouns and adjectives coupled with an ampersand. Examples would be Flint & Tinder, Hatch & Hops, Flour & Branch, Please & Stop, Seriously & Knock It Off.

It's not that this is a bad naming convention overall. It ticked some boxes of sparking intrigue and having a differentiated convention, at first. The issue is that all the kids ran towards the ball with feet kicking. Now you can't drive through a commercial district without seeing a few of these brands spanning everything from hair care to restaurants.

Note: The irony of having named our blog Grits & Grids is not lost on me. I'll happily accept taunts, prods, and jokes.

Naming is hard, but it can be done without the help of an agency. Although I do suggest getting professional help with developing your brand name. If not for any other reason except you have plenty of other things to do—that only you can do. Why not let bakers bake the bread?

What Makes for a Great Name?

Wildly successful brand naming stems from being unique and noteworthy while evoking a brand's personality in a profound way. A brand name should act as a concise entry point to a deeper story, meaning, and purpose that can be found throughout the many nuances of the brand and its experiences. It must spark intrigue to learn more to create that patron buy-in to immerse further into the brand's nuances.

There are some guidelines for creating brand names that work, but it's also a pretty open, undiscovered land of opportunity. From one side, I will urge that a brand name is extremely important, and at the same time tell you that it's not THAT important. What I mean by that is you cannot afford to have a name that works against potential success. It cannot misinform the Patron or create an expectation that doesn't align with what the brand delivers on.

At the same time, putting too much emphasis on the name's role in success is unfair. It creates an uphill climb in search of "the perfect name," and that may result in discouragement or skepticism over a name that will do quite well. A lot of times clients of ours have been hoping for an "aha!" moment with naming workstreams, only to be disappointed when it doesn't happen. That doesn't mean the proposed names aren't fantastic or won't create a successful brand. It just means that the expectations were off.

In order to develop and identify a great name for a brand, one must have the right mindset. Here is a list of truths to help guide expectations and get you and whatever team you're working with in the right headspace to develop a name that will make competitors jealous.

Names are rarely encountered without context.

The most common feedback received during naming is, "that doesn't sound like a restaurant," or "that sounds like a [blank]." Both derive from the same limbic, or gut, reaction that's influenced by prototypes or conventions that exist currently. Allowing this to influence the name of the restaurant is a fast-track to mediocrity and the land of forgettable brands.

Names are rarely experienced without context, meaning there will be elements influencing perceptions. Whether it's graphic design, explanation in conversation, or audio delivery mechanisms, the name absorbs the context and guides the perception. This means that a name like "Banana Republic" won't conjure notions of a crippled island economy, and will, instead, take on new meaning.

Context is everything. It's what defines, or redefines, a name, giving it new life and intrigue.

Existing brands should be used to evaluate the viability or feasibility of a brand name.

It's easy to look to brands that currently exist as benchmarks for good names—or bad ones. This is a mistake for a few reasons.

First, the brand's name plays only a small role in the success of a restaurant. Finances, operations, and marketing all work in unison to determine the fate of a restaurant brand. Your brand's name can drastically help or slightly hinder the chances of success.

Secondly, the restaurants that exist today were started in a different time, sometimes era. The competitive landscape and sociocultural climate were different, meaning the brand's name was born and raised differently.

Finally, emulating an existing name only results in a brand that's poised to be perceived as a ripoff or "me too." That never works. For example, no brand will be a better Panera than Panera itself.

A name will not and should not tell the whole story of a brand.

Oftentimes, a brand name is expected to tell the whole story, or at least one that's much more lengthy. This, too, is a mistake. Just as your personal name cannot tell your entire story, neither can a restaurant's brand name. It's impossible, and therefore attempting to accomplish this is an exercise in futility.

A name cannot tell the whole story, because your story is complex. It's made up of many facets and nuances across many touchpoints. Asking a name to fulfill this desire creates unnecessary expectations that make it near impossible to find a name that works.

Names do not have to be easy to pronounce or spell.

You may be shaking your head in disbelief, but this is true within reason. We certainly don't want a name that's impossible to pronounce or spell. However, a name that has some pronunciation or spelling hurdles isn't a bad thing. Here's why:

Humans are a "tribe" culture and revel in acquiring knowledge that's not massively proliferated. It gives people a sense of belonging. Pronunciation and spelling offer a sense of belonging, which taps the need to be a part of a tribe.

Spelling won't prevent someone from finding or falling in love with a brand. Google's ability to predict and suggest helps guide people in the right direction.

Lack of availability in digital or social media real estate should not eliminate an otherwise viable name.
Although it would be ideal to have a URL that reflects your brand exactly as it's written, the chances of this are very low. The impossibility is compounded when seeking to establish commonality across all digital touchpoints (e.g., Twitter, Instagram handles.)

People are accustomed to URLs that aren't solely the brand's name plus "dot com." In fact, it poses a great opportunity to inject personality. For instance, "eatrestaurant.com" versus "dinerestaurant.com." Both are essentially the same, but shape perceptions in different directions.

The lack of availability should not discourage an otherwise fantastic name. Get creative and make that name work with a URL and social handle suite that are brand-centric.

Some people will hate the brand's name.
Actually, some people will dislike your concept, too. The fact is, the generalist approach may feel like it's the best opportunity for maximal growth, but it's the opposite. You cannot please everyone.

If you try to be everything to everyone, you'll become nothing to anyone. The key to success is owning a niche and pushing it brazenly and indelibly. Be unafraid of your brand, its offering, and the attitude you put into the world. You may make some people dislike you, but you'll have even more who love you. Brand love is the root of brand leadership and loyalty.

Steer clear of outside feedback.

In the same vein as liking and disliking the name, it's important to note that asking for outside opinions will result in a forgettable name and brand. People react to what they already know. They are not innovators at heart and will automatically push back on what's unfamiliar. Henry Ford famously stated, "If I had asked people what they wanted, they would have said faster horses." However, the right questions and observations with potential customers can yield powerful insights.

The key is to ensure the person is in the brand's core audience and that the questions are objective in nature. Questions like "do you like this?" Or "what do you think of this?" won't return valuable information. Instead, questions like "What does this name convey to you?" will get tangible information that can be used to create strong names and even stronger brands. Everyone has an opinion; not all of them are useful.

If we had to break down two benchmarks that make for a great brand name, they would be:

1. **A brand's name must be distinctive.** If hard-pressed to make a singular profound statement about what a brand name should be, "distinctive" would be it. "Distinctive"

is defined as, characteristic of one person or thing, and so serves to distinguish it from others.

That is the most crucial ask for a name. A distinctive name will get attention. It gets remembered. When tied to brand experiences equally distinctive and aligned through a passionate purpose, the brand solidifies as best in class.

2. **A brand's name must create intrigue and conversation.** The best names aren't the ones that fall into the monotony with sameness. They're the ones that spark conversation. They beg a question that prompts experiences to answer and dig deeper. When the stories connect with the name, magic happens. A brand name should be distinctive enough to get people talking and asking questions. Then, and only then, will they be primed for immersive experiences.

Names that follow these guidelines are primed to get attention and engagement. They're poised to create the intrigue necessary to break through the highly competitive brandscape. They're primed to win.

Four Examples of Fantastic Restaurant Brand Names

At this point, your head may be spinning from the theory and thinking. You may be asking, "Great, so what's that look and sound like?" Well, fear not my friend, here are a few names that we think tick the boxes of distinction and intrigue:

I'm Eddie Cano

When I encountered this name I was intrigued. I was approached by a reporter from *The Washingtonian* who specifically wanted our take on the name. What seemed like an interesting convention quickly had me chuckling. When rapidly spoken, the name changes immediately as it sounds like "Americano" in an Italian accent. Go ahead, try it out.

That fun quirk ties directly to the approach to the food at I'm Eddie Cano. It's fun, neighborly, and has a streak of authenticity without presumption. I absolutely love this name and think it's a winner, but I dislike the brand's identity. The core logo draws the link between the name and the pronunciation, losing the tribal membership factor and killing that serendipitous moment where the name's meaning clicks. Furthermore, the naming inspiration and convention aren't found anywhere else throughout the experience. That's a big miss. But at least they got the name right.

My Neighbor Felix

One of my favorite names that has been developed by my team at Vigor is for a modern pan-Mexican, full-service restaurant in Denver, Colorado. The name My Neighbor Felix takes on an interesting composition that's unfamiliar in the restaurant space. That uniqueness creates a level of distinction that drives a person to learn more. When they peel back the layers, they're met with a deeper meaning that connects with the Patron's values.

"Neighbor" directly connects to the sense of belonging and togetherness the restaurant looks to foster while developing a subtle correlation to the geographic placement of the country of Mexico. "Felix" is a neighborly name but also has ties to good luck in the

Spanish language. And the word "My" instills an instant feeling of ownership. Collectively, it grabs attention and delivers meaning that's reinforced and developed across the brand's touchpoints.

Hidden Rhythm

Created by our friends at A Hundred Monkeys, this food events company was born from a passionate blog called Confetti Kitchen. That passion grew into a food events business that looked to shed the cringey cuteness of the blog and introduce a sense of unusual mystique aligned with the events' diverse experiences.

"Right off the bat, it felt unusual and unexpected. As namers, we love joining two words that aren't typically used together — they reverberate and they allow us to build meaning around them, creating a world of possibility and ownability, not to mention intrigue," states Eli Altman on the case studies web page.[36]

From the very moment one encounters this name, the intrigue sets in. It doesn't say anything about "events" or "planning." It doesn't need to. It grips a person with a distinctiveness and curiosity to dive in deeper and immerse in the social or digital touchpoints where one can develop a deeper understanding and belief in Hidden Rhythm's offering and brand.

Brick River Cider Co.

Another Vigor creation, Brick River Cider Co. continues to strike me as a poetic name. Brick River is St. Louis, Missouri's first cider company, and the founder's passion for connecting cities back to

---

[36] Eli Altman, "Cute no More," A Hundred Monkeys, accessed April 15, 2021, https://www.ahundredmonkeys.com/brand/hidden-rhythm-2/.

their agrarian roots. His belief, and the belief instilled throughout the brand, is that there exists a delicate, symbiotic relationship between cities and countrysides that should not be forgotten. It should be celebrated.

The name is a mixture of many meanings. Bricks have been a main export of St. Louis, a city that garnered the nickname, "The Brick City" as a result. The mighty Mississippi River runs through the city, and the midwestern United States, opening up the ability to realize heavy commerce in an otherwise landlocked area. The "Muddy River" has a brick hue to it, but that's not the only correlation to the brand name.

The brand's name is a metaphor for the pathways that led farmers to city centers. A river of bricks, or a road, is what connected the cities to their agricultural systems, serving as a critical link between town and country. Pure poetry in my opinion.

These four names are simply examples, but the world is full of amazing brand names (and plenty more terrible ones.) Your brand name is quite possibly the first thing a Patron will encounter. Better make sure it's distinctive and intriguing because you don't get a second chance to make a successful first impression.

Beyond the Logo: Think Visual Language

A brand's logo is only one small component of a much larger ecosystem. And this is what makes a logo simultaneously important and not that important. Everyone knows a company needs a logo. It's a core component of communicating the brand to the world. The logo exists across many touchpoints in the brand's Presentation layer and serves as its epicenter. Therefore, the logo has a big job to do. But, the logo isn't alone in its endeavor to communicate a brand's nuances and details to the world. That's where a lot of folks go wrong.

In many cases, a leader will commission the design of a logo, then proceed to slap that logo everywhere possible. From the signage to t-shirts and packaging to interiors, the brand's logo is thoughtlessly slapped wherever possible, and it's called "branding." That approach is stupid, wrong, and very much not branding.

A brand's visual identity consists of many other components that collectively work to communicate the brand's details. Colors, typography, imagery styles, patterns, and other visual artifacts serve to add nuance to the brand's Presentation layer.

The core logo itself can be broken down into secondary iterations for use where a full logo would be overkill. Secondary logos can be monograms, simple marks, emblems, and more (see figure 03). These secondary items add to a system of visual communications that create a visual language. And that's the key to effective identity design.

Wikipedia defines a language as "a structured system of communication used by humans, including speech (spoken language), gestures (sign language) and writing. Most languages have a writing system composed of glyphs to inscribe the original sound or gesture and its meaning."[37] We can expand on this definition to include a system of shapes, colors, and typographical elements that visually communicate a brand's personality.

---

[37] "Language," Wikipedia, last modified April 11, 2021, https://en.wikipedia.org/w/index.php?title=Language&oldid=1017267977.

fig. 03

PRIMARY

PANANOVA
craft kitchen

SECONDARY MARKS

PRIMARY VARIANTS

PANANOVA
craft kitchen

PANANOVA
FRESH *craft kitchen* FAST

When one thinks of a brand's identity as a language, vast opportunities open up to create a deeper, more profound experience. No longer do you have the urge to slap the same logo everywhere. Instead, one may opt to use a secondary mark on the menu since most folks will know where they are and will have encountered the core logo multiple times. Uniforms can be designed with the brand's typography to push forth one-liner sayings that evoke the brand's verbal identity (we'll get into that shortly.) Or maybe they take cues from the brand's identity to develop an illustrative style that's employed across the system.

Approaching the brand's full Presentation layer with a visual language in mind creates an experience in line with the advanced complexity of today's consumers. People are much more mentally and emotionally advanced today than they were even ten years ago. They're uber-connected through technologies that feed them impressive amounts of data minute-by-minute from podcasts to audiobooks, social-media feeds to news feeds. Our capacity for learning and knowledge has astronomically expanded year by year.

You can see this play out in other media-like television programs and feature-length motion pictures. Gone are the days of the classic sitcom where the hero of the show would encounter a problem, it'd reach a melting point, then the day is saved and lessons are learned all within a 30-minute time-frame. No, we're in an era where a television program can have twenty different characters with seemingly contrasting storylines that work their way towards intersection over ten seasons. And people follow it and want more.

Just as a classic sitcom has very little traction today, so does a classic approach to brand-identity design. People want more. They want to immerse and dive in. They want to see something new around every corner and on every wall. And what they see should be orchestrated with a common thread that creates a full experience and consistent narrative. That is the core of successful visual identity design.

As stated earlier, every single part of the brand is an opportunity to push the narrative further. Go beyond utility and think about opportunity. While the logo is important, it is only one of many components of a strong identity. Stop expecting so much from it, and start developing a more robust language that works to communicate the brand everywhere possible.

Four Hallmarks of a Strong Visual Identity

What makes a visual identity great? This may be one of the hardest questions to answer because the design can be quite subjective. Despite going to school for design, and constantly learning about design trends, one can find that it's not a discipline that subscribes to objective rules like that of architecture. While there do exist principles of design that, when followed, can ensure a good result, those rules can be broken and still result in something quite remarkable. This makes evaluating design very difficult.

Design is a mix of art and science. It's an applied art, meaning it has a function, and that function is to communicate. If one distills down the purpose of visual identity, and what makes a visual identity great, it would be this: to effectively communicate a brand's platforms in a way that differentiates it from competing brands. That purpose is accomplished by leveraging every touchpoint available to a brand.

A visual identity begins with the design of a logo. A natural byproduct of that endeavor are design elements that aren't fit for the core logo but could be great additions to the overall language. Additionally, in designing the logo, two core outputs occur: color palette and typography.

Both the color palette and typography get their start in the design of a logo, but that's not the beginning and the end. The colors chosen for the logo serve as the start of a color palette, but that palette can, and oftentimes should, expand into more colors.
The same goes for the brand's typography. While the logo design introduces one or two typography elements, they may not be the only type families used throughout the full visual identity language. In fact, using the typeface found in the core logo may be a bad move altogether.

As one designs the visual identity elements, the language starts to form. And that language is what inevitably becomes set in stone as the brand's standards. Those standards serve as a guide and a rulebook for how to design and create new touchpoints. It's the basis for the meaning of the terms "off brand" and "on brand" which you may hear a design partner or brand manager state over and over again.

Off brand means that the visual or verbal composition in question is not adhering to one or many standards set forth by the brand's standards. In this case, the offending elements must be rethought or adjusted to meet the standards as outlined.

To be "on brand" is the goal of every touchpoint. Even if that touchpoint introduces a new design element or a new piece of copy, they should adhere to the standards. When this happens, the touchpoint is added as another moment that effectively, consistently communicates the brand to anyone who may encounter it. In the process, it adds another reason to believe the brand's claims and promises creating trustworthiness and ushering Patrons close to advocacy.

But what makes a "great identity" design? What are some of the hallmarks? While we cannot possibly cover every nuance of what defines great design, we can cover four hallmarks of a great identity. They are as follows:

Must be distinctive.
This may sound like a "well duh" statement, but it has to be said. A successful visual identity is uniquely different from competing brands. From colors through copy it sets the brand into a league of its own, and in the process, it draws attention, sparks intrigue, and invites viewers in to learn more and dig deeper.

Distinctiveness may be one of the toughest hallmarks to achieve because it goes against human inclination to belong or assure success. We tend to be attracted to the familiar. It provides confirmation that something will work. It "feels" right because it has been seen before, whether we cognitively realize it or not. But familiarity is a death sentence for brands. Yup, I'll write it again, if you spend your time trying to fit in, you'll waste your budget trying to stand out. Dare to be distinctive.

Must communicate the Personality.

Yes, there are many other layers of the Golden Lasso that must be communicated, but it's impossible for a visual identity to effectively communicate them all. There exists a myriad of other touchpoints where those layers, namely the Purpose and Product, can and will be communicated. Therefore, the laser focus for a visual language must be to communicate and evoke the brand's unique Personality traits. It should feel like those traits through and through.

Think of a visual language as clothing and accessories on a person as they arrive at a party. You can tell a lot about the way a person dresses, or at least, a lot about what they want you to think about them. Hello, Patron Projection layer! When walking into a room of women in little black dresses, wearing a little black dress would feel very comforting. In this scenario, it would be extremely difficult for a woman in a little black dress to stand out and get attention. However, if we switch the color of the dress, that woman is immediately at an attention-getting advantage. It may not feel comfortable to be dressed counter to the masses, but we're not in the game of comfort, remember?

What color dress should our anecdotal woman wear? Well, that's driven by her personality. If she's fiery, sultry, and bold, a red dress would be a great statement. If she's fun, quirky, and upbeat, maybe a floral chintz print dress would fit the bill. It is the garment that communicates her intended personality, just like our brand's visual identity evokes the brand's personality.

Must be consistent.

Consistency is key to believability and trust. A brand's suite of touchpoints must be consistent in order to cultivate that trust and usher Patrons towards loyalty and advocacy. Any area where consistency is lacking to any degree is a weak point that deteriorates brand believability.

Inconsistency can be found everywhere in even the most successful brands. It happens when a partner or vendor doesn't care enough to review, understand, and follow the brand standards. It happens when leaders shirk the responsibility of understanding the weight of brand consistency and owning the brand standards. I don't know how many times I've seen a restaurant sign that clearly uses the wrong typeface, or the logo has been squished to fit into a certain area. It's cheap and ugly and it negatively affects brand perceptions.

It is the job of everyone inside the company to introduce and enforce the brand's standards. No exceptions. The goal for all involved is to not just tick the boxes of on-brand evaluations, but to find ways to bolster and build the brand through new expressions that adhere to the standard but grow its reach.

Must be documented.

Consistency is born out of strong, concise documentation. That document is called a Brand Standards Book or Guide or a Brand

6. Presentation

Manual. This document, which can be digital, physical, or both, is essentially a detailed guide that outlines the standards of the brand.

A best-in-class brand-standards guide introduces and outlines in great detail the following elements of the brand:

- ☐ The strategic platforms with further details to foster understanding

- ☐ The core brand logo with associated narrative and explanations design elements

- ☐ Appropriate and inappropriate variations of the logo from color to composition

- ☐ Logo's clear space, or how much space around the logo should be kept clear of any other design element

- ☐ Secondary logos and brand marks and how they are to be used

- ☐ Colors in the brand's palette with codes to be used in print and digital applications

- ☐ Typography to be used for visual communications along with each typeface's use cases (e.g., headlines, body copy, etc.)

- ☐ Slogan and/or headline treatments

- ☐ Patterns, iconography, and other graphic elements

- ☐ Illustration and photography styles

☐ Applications of the brand in use as examples of correct usage

A brand standards guide should cover as much detail as possible to foster a deep understanding of the brand's strategic foundations and the rules on how to express that brand across channels and touchpoints. As the brand grows and evolves, the guide should be updated and adjusted accordingly. Therefore, a successful brand standards guide is one that is alive and prepared to grow, just like the brand itself.

A distinctive, consistent, well-documented visual identity that evokes the brand's personality is the most powerful tool for every brand and its leadership. It is the core of the brand's Presentation layer. Without it, brand experiences rely on gut feeling and the whims of leadership's personal tastes to dictate how the brand manifests and presents itself. It creates a hodge-podge experience wrought with inconsistencies and reason to disbelieve the brand's claims and promises. It is not only a chink in the armor, it's a gaping hole waiting to be exploited to the detriment of the business.

Therefore, it's important to treat the visual identity and the brand guidebook that houses its details, as a Bible for your brand's communications. This is your brand's sacred cow.

To download an example of a brand standards manual, please visit bullhearted.co/brand-manual

Menu Design: What's on the Menu?

Effective menus do more than list out the available items. Whether it's a fine dining, white-glove iconoclast of luxury or a fast-food, convenience, and price-driven powerhouse, the menu systems are critical to realizing maximum ticket averages as well as delivering on the brand's personality and purpose. But so often, companies and designers opt for a plunk and dunk approach to menu design giving little attention to the opportunities to weave in a narrative and engineer the menu design for sales optimization.

Additionally, there are prevalent "rules" when it comes to menu design that hinder the ability to realize a best-in-class brand experience. Figurative Sacred Cow Alert! One of the most prevalent that I've encountered is the argument that fine dining restaurants can't have pictures on the menu because it looks cheap. False! Beautiful photography is an art form on its own, and beautiful photography can not only create an upscale vibe on a menu, it can also increase sales of profitable and perception driving items, and that's a core goal for a successful menu.

A successful menu realizes profitability while driving and guiding brand perceptions. They focus on a mix of profitability, popularity, and perceptual drivers to create an experience that maximizes sales without impeding the utility of needing to find and order what a Patron wants. In order to realize this balance, it's important to approach menu design with engineering first. After all, form does follow function. You're welcome, architect pals.

Before jumping into any design-related initiatives, it is my belief that the menu be engineered for success. Menu engineering is primarily a numbers game. Industry best practices dictate that a menu be analyzed using the four quadrants of the traditional Boston Consulting Group's Growth-Share Matrix. Those quadrants were originally: Stars, Cash Cows, Question Marks, and Pets.[38] Over the years, the restaurant industry has evolved them into: Stars, Puzzles, Plowhorses, and Dogs. They are defined as such:

- ☐ Stars are the items that see the highest popularity with the most profitability.

- ☐ Puzzles have high profitability but aren't very popular.

- ☐ Plowhorses are highly popular, but not profitable.

- ☐ Dogs are neither popular nor profitable.

Getting a handle on how your menu breaks down in these quadrants is crucial. The goal is to continue to bolster the Stars while making adjustments to usher Puzzles and Plowhorses towards becoming Stars. Plowhorses should be engineered to have lower food cost without cutting quality, while Puzzles could be pushed with marketing endeavors to increase their popularity. Additionally, Puzzles can be uplifted through menu design.

The inclination to remove all Dogs is a tough one to combat. Why keep items that make little money and aren't very popular? There is one reason to not remove them outright: brand perceptions. Some Dogs may have a purpose on a menu despite not directly doing much for the bottom-line. If an item on the menu helps uplift or guide the perception of the other menu items, then that item has a case for staying on. A good example of this is with TGI Friday's menu from a few years ago.

---

[38] "What is the Growth Share Matrix?" Boston Consulting Group, accessed April 15, 2021, https://www.bcg.com/about/our-history/growth-share-matrix.

Friday's introduced sriracha ahi tuna nachos onto the appetizer menu. Then president, Nick Sheppard, told me directly that that menu item was neither popular nor profitable, but they kept it on because it gave valuable context to the other items. The existence of that menu item positively affected the perceptions of quality and culinary acumen to the other surrounding items. While it was still a Dog, that Dog had a metaphoric bite.

Obviously, it's impossible to evaluate a menu for a startup brand since there is no data on popularity. In this instance, the menu should be evaluated to identify the profitable items and the items you think will drive perceptions of the offering.

There are good reasons why menu engineering is a discipline on its own. A well engineered menu can help a restaurant realize optimum levels of success and revenue.

Menu Design: What's the Menu On?

With the analytical work conducted, the design of the menu systems can begin, starting with identifying what types of menus are required for the brand experience. With standard quick-service restaurants the menu systems consist of menuboards, handheld, and possibly a drive-thru menu. For full service, the system gets larger. Full-service restaurants can have any number of menus covering their offering from a single menu that contains everything to multiple menus for each daypart and offering.

In both cases, each menu in the system usually consists of two parts: the element that physically holds the menu, and the element that contains the menu content. For handheld menus, this is a combination of a menu holder and the inserts that go into the holder. For menuboards, it's the physical elements that affix to the wall or ceiling, combined with the content applied to those boards. Lately, these have become digital screens, but the system for holding them still must be determined, and there is room for design innovation to create board systems evocative of the brand's personality.

Every part of the menu system should be considered through the brand lens. Visually it must bolster and build the brand's identity. The items that are handheld offer an opportunity to accentuate the brand's personality by considering the tactile experience. For instance, leather and other textiles can uplift the perceptions of luxury. Thick paper that has texture can also create and guide a brand experience in line with the Personality layer.

Once the mechanisms have been identified, consider their design through the brand lens. How can this be molded and designed to be another remarkable piece of the brand experience? Hint: Slapping the logo on the front isn't a winner here. Instead, the entire piece should be considered and designed to evoke the brand's personality. Maybe that means a subtle emblem—gold foil stamped into the bottom right corner. Maybe that means a menu that lets the materials speak on the outside, and on the inside introduces a surprising composition that delivers the brand's narrative. This is a moment to push the boundaries and really flex that brand communication opportunity.

Building from the menu holder design, the menu inserts are considered next. This is where the engineering comes into play while also introducing more brand elements into the visual language. Menus can be quite lengthy so a designer will need to leverage graphic elements that divide up content for easier visual consumption. Additionally, the Stars and Puzzles of the menu should be elevated with design techniques to draw people's eyes towards them and drive sales.

The overall design of the menu should be driven by the brand's standards. However, it does serve as an opportunity to grow the standards with guidelines for long-form content, including heading structures and callout styles. Even how the pricing is displayed should be considered and then set as a brand standard. As the menu insert layouts come to life, designers should consider eye movement to maximize the experience.

Be warned, while I believe that eye-tracking can be powerful, it can also be a bit of a waste of time because every menu and every concept is different. For instance, eye tracking on a quick-service drive-through menu board is much different than a fine dining handheld experience. Figurative Sacred Cow Warning: Be careful when relying on prevalent knowledge on eye-tracking as it can be misleading.

Oh, and don't forget the chit, also known as the check presenter! This is a huge opportunity to finish the experience with a unique, on-brand moment of surprise and delight. Check presenters can be anything from a beautifully designed postcard that a guest can take with them, to a refined, elegant portfolio that showcases the level of craft the brand wishes to convey. Even the receipt itself should be considered if the technology allows. Imagine having a receipt designed through the lens of the brand's identity. Now that's something worth looking at!

The menu suite is a highly immersive opportunity to bring the brand to life. It not only serves as a mechanism for driving sales, it also guides overall brand perceptions. When done right, it will deliver on the brand's promise, tell the brand's story, and maximize ticket averages while setting expectations. Your team just has to exceed them with stellar service and remarkable food, even if you're a QSR.

For menu design inspiration, check out Grits & Grids at www.gritsandgrids.com.

Location, Location, Location

There's a reason this real estate slogan has stuck through the decades and across business categories. Location is everything when it comes to restaurants, and the location says a lot about the brand itself. The neighborhood and surrounding areas help influence and guide the perceptions of the brand. Additionally, the type of real estate can influence how people perceive a brand.

For instance, imagine a white glove, high-end fine dining restaurant flanked in a strip mall by a Walmart and a vape shop. Suddenly the level of "fine" and "high-end" is very much in question. Alternatively, imagine a quick-service restaurant that sells tacos and promotes affordability but exists in the bottom of a Ritz Carlton in the most expensive neighborhood in town. It's hard to attract the Patrons looking for cheap, fast food in a glamorously expensive neighborhood.

All of this may seem like common sense, but if there's one thing I've learned in the business of restaurants is that a lot of times "sense" goes out the door for all sorts of reasons. So best to clearly state it and reinforce it rather than hoping you, the reader, already knows it.

For most restaurants, a prime location is ideal. Prime locations position the restaurant in a place where there is plenty of foot traffic from both residential, commercial, and tourism throughout all parts of the day. They have easy access to parking that's convenient to find and get in and out of. They are flanked by retailers and companies that accentuate the brand's offerings and attract the same Patrons. Starting to sound a bit like a fairytale?

That may be the case. Finding a prime location, let alone multiple prime locations, for a restaurant is not easy. That's why there are leaders who have this as a sole focus. It can be more than a full-time job to scout, research, and analyze potential locations looking for the right mix of variables that will position the brand for success.

While commercial real estate agents can be helpful, some don't have their client's best interests in mind. Finding a trustworthy, effective commercial real estate agent can be just as hard as finding the real estate itself. I've seen many brands get sold on spaces destined for failure and there's little to no recourse. So if you had ideas that your real estate guy or gal is going to get you sorted, think again.

One would think that all prime locations lead to success, but that's not the case. I've personally seen a number of restaurants find success in obscure, off-the-beaten-path-locations. The obscurity taps a sense of tribalism in the Patron that's highly effective in creating intrigue and allure. There's a sense of "if you know you know" that sparks curiosity in folks, creating the kindling for a grassroots type of brand building.

In these cases, the restaurant must be offering a fully developed brand experience that fires on all cylinders. From the food and flavor through the interiors and exteriors, the whole brand must work in concert to tell the story and communicate a narrative that makes sense with having an off-the-beaten-path location. When done right, it can be a highly effective marketing strategy to fuel the word of mouth necessary to get the brand to catch on.

If you're launching a new brand, you're going to be dropping some serious money investing in its strategy, design, and development. For this reason, I do suggest that leaders of new concepts look for second-generation spaces. By "second generation" I mean spaces that have already been occupied by a restaurant that has chosen to vacate or has failed.

The reason for this suggestion is that the original restaurant and property owner will have already invested in the heavy lifting to fit the space for the restaurant format, reducing the cost of opening. Just because another restaurant has come and gone doesn't mean the space doesn't have value. However, if that restaurant has failed, you'd be wise to do enough research to learn why and avoid going down the same path to failure.

I cannot stress enough how important it is to not jump into the first deal that strikes your fancy. Nor should you fall in love with a spot and let it dictate your brand unless that's your business model. The brand's strategy should influence where you open up new locations, so use it wisely and be prepared to walk away from what seems like a great deal. Because if it doesn't align with your brand, it's not going to work and you'll become another addition to the high-failure statistics.

Four Walls, Limitless Opportunities

By far the biggest investment for restaurants is in the design and build. The cost of labor and materials is astronomical, but the return on the investment is well worth it. The interiors of a restaurant are where all the promises, all the marketing, and all communications come to life. In this space, the brand must deliver on what's been promised and overdeliver to create moments of elation. The opportunities to do that are only limited by imagination, budget, and desire.

As with every touchpoint in a restaurant's brand experience, interiors and architecture have both form and function. It's absolutely critical that the function of a space be considered before any elements of form. Ensuring people can get to where they need and want, and teams can find what they need in as little time as possible is key to creating a remarkable experience both inside and outside the company. Once that function has been effectively addressed and understood, the form can start to be developed.

Developed is the right word for the job. Creating interior experiences isn't simply about finding nice textiles and cool furniture. It's not an exercise in paint colors and finishes. While all of those elements play a role in creating an immersive space, without Purpose driving forward ideation and inspiration, it's simply decoration. Decoration has no place in design because it rests solely on the whims of people's personal tastes.

A brand's interiors are the number one place to evoke its Personality and continue to build on the brand's identity. And yet, the opportunities are poorly activated or missed altogether because designers fail to see the correlation between brand and interior design, or they genuinely don't understand said correlation.

To many interior designers, branding is the logo, and if you just put the logo on a wall or two the brand has been activated. That's lazy at best and negligent at worst. Interior designers' failure to understand what a brand is and how it drives design decisions is tragic and dangerous. My suggestion to anyone working with a designer who seems to not understand branding is to politely walk away no matter how good their portfolio may be.

Aesthetically pleasing design isn't enough to create an immersive experience. Designers and the clients who lead them should have a full understanding of the brand's strategy and identity standards. A great designer can find parallels between the brand's visual identity and actual finishes creating links to other touchpoints throughout the brand experience. When that happens, the interiors become even more powerful immersion points.

When we took on the rebranding initiative for a small bagel café in Lexington, Kentucky, the client wasn't one hundred percent sure of how they wanted to approach the interiors. After engaging in a highly successful rebranding workstream, their trust had fully formed, and we were awarded the project.

Our team collaborated to design a beautiful-looking space that was fully evocative of the brand's Personality, Purpose, and visual identity. We found parallels in graphic patterns that we had created in the identity design workstream with physical textures and finishes.

For instance, the brand's visual identity featured diagonally patterned wheat line art that served as a linear pattern used on windows and the bottoms of the menus. We matched this pattern to a herringbone orientation of wood floor planks to create a subtle connection between the two elements. Another example was our use of a LED ring pendant chandelier that mimicked the halo found in the brand's logo.

Nowhere in the space did we showcase the brand's core logo. Instead, we activated and extended the brand's visual language to create a unique space that was undeniably owned by that brand. From murals to menu systems, we were able to bring the brand to life and live the brand's purpose.

A good way to evaluate whether or not an interior experience is effectively evoking the brand is by simply removing any logo elements within the space and replacing them with another brand. If the new brand works well with the space, then that's a good indicator that the design, although pretty, is generic and not unique enough to present as a brand immersion point.

Yes, form does follow function, but that's not to discount the importance of form. In fact, form has its own function: to communicate the brand's personality and purpose in ways that are remarkable and unique. When successfully accomplished, the interiors are unforgettable and highly attractive to Patrons, which leads to word of mouth, repeat traffic, and growth. There are limitless opportunities to realize this level of design, so long as leadership and trusted partners understand the brand's strategy and how to effectively push it forward within the space.

Digital Is as Important as Physical

I remember the days when websites were a new thing and a lot of restaurants weren't sure if they needed them. Yeah, I'm that old. Jumping to today, restaurants know they need one, but they still don't like to pay very much for them. Yet they expect a lot from their websites and are frustrated when they don't deliver the desired effects.

Websites play a critical role in telling a restaurant's story while delivering on the utility of driving sales. Whether it's in the form of online ordering or reservations, the ultimate benchmark for success is in converting site visitors to revenue. But a simple button in the navigation isn't enough to effectively reach that goal. They are as important as the physical space because they deliver a highly immersive experience that can be just as deep and profound.

As with the interiors, restaurant brands have big opportunities when it comes to their websites. Sure, they could throw up the menu and some pictures, add in a logo, and call it a day, but that type of website is essentially a boring brochure. Nobody wants to visit a site like that. And because Google has done such a stellar job at aggregating data, people really don't need to visit a brand's site.

Think about it, in Google, you can find the restaurant's location, reviews, menu information, hours of operation, and photographs of the food all with one search. So why would anyone bother visiting a website that delivers no more than those baseline elements? They won't. At least not more than once. Yet restaurants still devalue the power and potential of their website, investing only enough to serve up exactly what Google's already delivering. Seems like a waste of time and money to me.

Instead of checking the box of utility, a website should be approached through the brand's strategic lens. Do I sound like a broken record yet? The brand's Personality and Purpose should drive ideation and collaboration on what the website should and could do. It should spark new thinking that dares to deliver more than basics to invite people in and get them to spend time with the brand. That is the true goal of a website in this day and age.

When people spend time with a brand, their chances of recall go up. The brand stays top of mind longer, and when that person encounters a marketing message, they are more likely to act. A website that's built to deliver on the brand's purpose gets visitors to spend time while delivering on that narrative.

The easiest way to build time spent with a brand is through video. Video is unbelievably accessible and attainable these days. What's more, is you don't have to spend six figures to gather great video content that's more than suitable for brand storytelling. In fact, and to the frustration of many a videographer, the new iPhone 11 takes fantastic 4k video that's perfect for this use case. We'll dive more into video in the next chapter.

Video isn't the only way to get more time from Patrons. There are many types of content that garner time from content surrounding stories that give proof to the Product layer to quizzes and other interactive elements that build belief in the Personality. With the web, if you can imagine it, chances are it can be built. It all comes down to time and budget, but if it's the right idea, the returns on the investment are amazing.

In 2016, I had the pleasure of leading Zaxby's digital marketing push while consulting with a global advertising agency. Zaxby's is a well-known southern restaurant brand that's a major player in the QSR chicken game. Competing against other well-known, beloved brands like Chick-Fil-A, Zaxby's has to stay on its toes to get attention and traction.

Under my leadership, we relaunched a new .com experience for the brand that integrated online ordering to the extent that their partner technology would allow. The new .com checked all the boxes: menu items front and center, search engine optimization in full effect, and a design that was evocative of the brand's personality. However, the site was missing features that truly tapped Zaxby's spirit of fun and offbeatness.

My team and I brainstormed and collaborated on features that would uplift the experience and get more time with the Patron. Video played a role in some of the effort, but the real driver of brand Personality and time was in the Saucenality quiz.

Zaxby's was all about flavor in both the food sense as well as the flavor found in every individual. As a way to celebrate Zaxby's love of flavor, we developed the Saucenality quiz. The quiz took the Patron through a series of personality-driven questions. The answers to which triggered an algorithm that combined Zaxby's actual sauces into a mix unique to the person's personality. These sauce combinations were delivered as portmanteau, oftentimes purposely forced, coupled with a short personality writeup.

The Saucenality quiz received a lot of use from Patrons. In the process, Zaxby's collected their information, by consent of course, while delivering on their brand promise. Additionally, the quiz tied the Patron to the Product, driving sales and introducing people to other flavors they may not have tried.

Websites can be so much more than brochures with links to

ordering. Restaurant leaders who embrace this opportunity can create highly sticky experiences that get talked about. That sparks word of mouth and repeat visitations which culminates in Patrons who are primed to become advocates.

Yes, you will invest more than a few thousand dollars, but to be honest it won't be as expensive as an interior space. It can, however, be just as effective in delivering the brand's purpose and personality in ways physical spaces cannot if one simply puts in the effort and recognizes the opportunity.

The Fifth Wall: Augmented and Virtual Reality

At the time of this writing, the world has yet to scratch the surface of augmented reality and virtual reality. While some have taken leaps forward, they are still wide open for exploration, and the brands that see this opportunity can become early adopters and receive great benefits.

Investopedia defines Augmented Reality, AR for short, as "an enhanced version of the real physical world that is achieved through the use of digital visual elements, sound, or other sensory stimuli delivered via technology."[39] In contrast, Virtual Reality, VR for short, is "a computer simulation of a real or imaginary system that enables a user to perform operations on the simulated system and

---

[39] Adam Hayes, "Augmented Reality," *Investopedia*, updated December 2, 2020, https://www.investopedia.com/terms/a/augmented-reality.asp#:~:text=Augmented%20reality%20%28AR%29%20is%20an%20enhanced%20version%20of,in%20mobile%20computing%20and%20business%20applications%20in%20particular.

shows the effects in real-time."[40]

AR has gained popularity and adoption through highly addictive mobile games like *Pokémon Go* where players can see 3D pokémon in the world around them through the lens of their phone. People quickly jumped onboard the game and got a taste of Augmented Reality and how magical it can be. Imagine looking at the world around you and seeing unusual and amazing things that have been added through this technology.

Until recently, Augmented Reality experiences were sort of difficult to get off the ground. People would have to have downloaded an app that has AR activated in order to experience the features. That's a difficult hurdle to overcome for restaurants. However, a number of things happened in 2010s and in 2020 that removed that barrier.

First, apps with extremely high adoption popularity introduced Augmented Reality features tied to selfies. Instagram and Snapchat launched many filters for people to use to alter their appearances from big doughy eyes to the visual of vomiting a rainbow when one opens their mouth (see figure 04). Vanity, as it turns out, is an awesome driver of adoption.

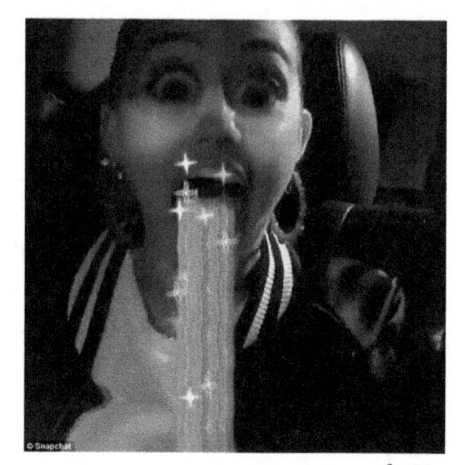

fig. 04

---

[40] *The American Heritage Dictionary of the English Language*, s.v. "virtual reality, https://www.ahdictionary.com/word/search.html?q=virtual+reality.

6. Presentation

In 2020, the world experienced a pandemic that changed many parts of daily life. One of the after-effects of the pandemic was the use and adoption of QR codes. QR, an abbreviation for "Quick Response," codes are scannable codes that open a link. For restaurants, this became the most sanitary way of delivering menu content and the preferred method during and post-pandemic. This basic action and need sparked high adoption rates of a technology that had been little used despite interest from marketers.

Coupled with newer software on phones that made scanning QR part of the system's phone, QR codes have realized the highest adoption rate ever. This fuels the ability to launch AR experiences as software and apps downloads aren't required, and people are accustomed to the actions to launch them.

For restaurants, there are boundless opportunities to take the experience to all new levels. No longer does one have to rely solely on the core senses to deliver a brand experience. Now another layer of reality can be applied to further drive home the brand's narrative.

Currently, we are working with our clients Vietvana on an augmented reality experience for their new location. As a guest approaches the stall at Ponce City Market, a renowned food hall in Atlanta, they encounter a beautiful space featuring posters and windows into the kitchen. Throughout the space, we are infusing QR codes that are strategically placed to spark intrigue.

When a Patron scans the codes, they launch unique, on-brand experiences. For instance, scanning a poster of a red-colored Buddha dancing with ingredients falling from the sky will launch a filter on Instagram that makes the person on camera red with the same ingredients falling all around them. Scanning the QR code near the area where the restaurant's house-made noodles are created will launch a filter that shows 3D noodles radiating around the head of the person on camera.

These filters are sure to spark word of mouth and usage from patron to patron. Furthermore, they naturally end up on social media feeds that are connected to the brand. This reach will fuel others to visit the location and play with the same features. The effects are as remarkable as the AR itself.

This is only one way AR can be used for restaurant brands. Imagine what can be done by augmenting the reality of the restaurant experience. I imagine a world where plating launches an experience that elevates the food and its story, or interior spaces that transport viewers to new worlds or new places. Those are just two potential experiences that could be created.

Virtual Reality has been around a lot longer, yet still does not have a large adoption rate. It's a heavier lift to create and integrate into an experience, but I have seen it done well. One way that strikes me as amazing was an experience launched by my friends at Zaxby's as a part of an event tour aligned with the NCAA.

In 2016, at predetermined college football games, Zaxby's set up a mobile experience in a shipping container. The brand was not allowed to sell food at these events, but they could still immerse people in Zaxby's magic. Using virtual reality and Facebook's Oculus hardware, Patrons were invited in to paint the Zaxby's mascot using their sauces.

We connected with the VR team to integrate it into a fuller campaign that we named Fanz of Flavor. This created a storyline that tied together the events, the virtual reality experience, Saucenality, and the launch of the brand's limited-time offer. The connectivity gave the campaign life outside of the VR experience, and leveraged it to spark curiosity amongst the brand's fans.

Brands and their creative teams should use the brand's strategy to ideate on what could be by daring to push the boundaries of reality. AR and VR offer up a world of opportunity to expand the experience and immerse patrons in remarkable moments. Whether it's as simple as activating AR filters for Instagram or launching fully immersive virtual reality experiences, these technologies are primed to change the game for restaurant brands today and into the future.

Activating the Brand with Internal Stakeholders

Activating the brand inside the company is just as important as activating it on the outside. It's the internal teams who have to deliver on the brand's strategy and continue to inject meaning into the brand through operations, product development, marketing, and more. That cannot happen without ensuring that everyone inside the organization understands and adopts the strategy and how it manifests on the Presentation layer. They just truly believe in the brand's Purpose in order to deliver on it. But that doesn't just happen naturally.

Effective brand activation is a top-down effort that's a never-ending endeavor. It is the job of leadership to practice and preach what the brand strategy means to the world inside and outside of the company. The people throughout the organization should not only be familiar with the brand's purpose, they should have full buy-in.

If anyone does not believe in that Purpose, leadership must make difficult decisions to replace that team member with someone who does.

Activation doesn't just happen with one meeting where the brand's strategy and identity are rolled out. While that's a fantastic opportunity to build excitement, it takes more than one interaction to garner buy-in. Instead, the brand should be activated through numerous channels and interactions with employees from top to bottom. Furthermore, as new team members join the company, they need to be introduced and onboarded. Therefore, activation is a journey and not a destination.

In my experience, activating the brand starts early. Since it's a top-down initiative, leaders who are engaged with the brand development process must understand that they will inevitably become the champions of the brand. They will be responsible for onboarding those around them, so full buy-in and unity are crucial.

As the team grows, or if there is already a team in place, the journey to developing the brand should be shared. Where possible, unity should be fostered as early as possible. If they feel engaged in the process, then they'll feel a sense of ownership.

Teams should understand why the organization is engaging in the brand development and the expected results. As the leadership team charges towards finalizing the strategy, the larger team should be introduced to the platforms. Then, when the visual and verbal identity are created, the whole package should be rolled out with as much fanfare as possible. This is especially true for rebrands.

After the initial launch, the company needs to create a presentation that can be used in the new hire onboarding process. This presentation should be engaging and interesting to ensure belief in the brand is fostered as quickly as possible. Combined with ongoing internal brand activation events, this should successfully create the buy-in necessary to create strong brand representation from the team.

The results of a successfully activated brand strategy span multiple areas of the business. Not only does it ensure the brand is believable by your Patron group, it also helps foster a great culture within the organization. Culture is highly valuable inside and outside the company, and it contributes to the quality of talent a brand can attract.

In today's restaurant industry, skilled talent is hard to find. Even more difficult is to find skilled talent that's eager to work and in love with your brand. Therefore, branding efforts have to focus on attracting, onboarding, and proliferating the brand's ideal inside the organization. Activating the brand and consistently fostering the understanding of the brand in the team will culminate in a culture that others want to join.

In Real Life: Simmering Down an Authentic Flavor of Sai Gon

In America, Vietnamese food maintains a cult-like following from city to city. Cultural staples such as pho and banh mi have gotten near mainstream attraction, but no Vietnamese concepts or brands have risen above mom-and-pop status. Some believe there is an allure created by the quaint, lo-fi experience found in those types of shops–something a refined look would take away. And so the look of Vietnamese restaurants are all pretty much the same. Cheap decor. Cheap furniture. Cheap food.

To make sure the food is approachable in price, shortcuts have been taken. To be fair, some of those shortcuts are due to a lack of access to original ingredients, but mostly it's driven by dollars and cents. No matter what drives that reality, it's a stark contrast to how food is prepared in Vietnam. And that was the source of inspiration for Khanh and Dinh, the husband and wife team who found themselves yearning for food as it's enjoyed on the streets of Sai Gon.

Khanh grew up in Vietnam and developed an acute taste for pho. When she immigrated to the United States, she found restaurants fell short of achieving the flavors she loved. When Khanh met Dinh, she explained that the pho here in the US was different. It tastes different. Together they set out on a journey to identify what made pho taste so different compared to that in Vietnam.

The answer was found in the noodles themselves. State-side, the majority of Vietnamese restaurants use pre-made noodles. The preservatives from those noodles noticeably alter the flavor of the Pho. And so the dream of bringing authentic pho to America was born.

As I outlined earlier in this book, "authentic" is a difficult word to own and uphold. But the founders were dead set on delivering a truly authentic experience. That started with the pho noodles.

For a few years, Dinh and Khanh worked with a third party to engineer and build a special machine that could output perfect, fresh pho noodles. Through trial and error, they finally realized their vision and shipped the machine from Vietnam to the shores of America. But the journey wasn't over.

Here in the States, people were accustomed to the altered flavor of pho. To them, it was how pho should taste. We had to tie the fresh pho noodles to authenticity and develop that understanding with the Patron group. We had to foster the feeling that this was pho on another level—a transcendent one. And thus was the beginning of the brand's strategy and the source of the brand's name: Vietvana.

Vietvana is a portmanteau of two words: Vietnam and Nirvana. Although "nirvana" is culturally associated with India, the term has been proliferated around the world to be associated with transcendence and the idea of an ultimate level of something. It is the goal of the Buddhist path and since Vietnam's dominant religion is Buddhism, the connection is authentic. For the restaurant, the name starts the conversation around the brand's purpose and belief: to realize the ultimate, authentic Vietnamese experience in the United States.

From that Purpose, we at Vigor designed the brand's visual and verbal identity to exalt the idea of authentic Vietnamese. Starting with the logo that was inspired by ink-stamped iconography through the bi-lingual touchpoints that unapologetically showcased Vietnamese language, the Vietvana brand seeks to own authenticity. But the visual identity's foundations were only the beginning.

We built upon the brand's visual identity with an illustrative style evocative of the French influence in Vietnam. The Art Deco illustrations merge the love of Vietnam and its food to tell a story of having started in Sai Gon. They are printed large and adorn the interiors with a breathtaking, eye-catching moment. They also serve as check presenters for those who are dining in. But it doesn't stop there.

The posters have an additional layer that has helped to proliferate the Vietvana brand even farther than imagined. We created and launched augmented reality (AR) experiences tied to the poster art. Patrons can scan a code on the poster and launch AR filters in Instagram to transform themselves into the poster art. Whether it's turning into a red buddha with ingredients falling all around, or suddenly wearing a nón lá (the iconic conical hat) and having noodles pull into one's mouth upon opening, the personality of Vietvana comes through in full effect.

Vietvana's brand personality influenced everything and helped tell the story of authenticity and what that means to the owners. At the time of this writing, Vietvana has two locations with another in the works. The brand is gathering momentum and building its foundation of brand advocates. The future is bright, and the owners couldn't be prouder of how far they've come and the path that lies before them.

Checkout the full Vietvana case study located at www.vigorbranding.com/projects/vietvana-vietnamese-restaurant-branding/

Recap & What's Next

At this point, you should have a full understanding of a brand's Golden Lasso. We have covered each platform that comprises the Golden Lasso strategy, why each element matters, and how it affects

7. Propelling Brands Ahead of the Herd

the others. With this clearly in view, you should be able to develop your own Golden Lasso strategy.

Once a strategy is completed, it then must be activated through marketing and design channels. In the next chapter, I'll outline how we propel brand's ahead through innovative, attention-grabbing creative and marketing strategies.

7. Propelling Brands Ahead of the Herd

Bull Story: Parade of Toritos

The Story

Every year at the beginning of March, something amazing happens in the municipality of Tultepec, Mexico. Craftspeople from Mexico's fireworks-maker industry gather to honor the patron saint of their craft, John of God, at the Feria Nacional de la Pirotecnia, or National Pyrotechnic Festival.

For seven days the people celebrate fireworks with amusement rides, concerts, dancing, and delicious food. There are three main events to the festival: the Contest of Castillos, Pamplonada, and a contest that merges fireworks and music. Of these events, the Pamplonada is the oldest and most important.

The Pamplonada honors the famous yearly Running of the Bulls in Pamplona, Spain with a pyrotechnic display involving bull-shaped frames affixed with fireworks. The frames are crafted from wood, reed, and hard paper mache called cartoneria. They're painted with vibrant colors and can range in size from four feet to nearly ten feet! The larger toritos, or little bulls, can showcase as many as 4,000 fireworks.

Each of the toritos are given names such as El Chico, Sagitario Toro Maya, and Monster. On March 8th, they ignite for 5-6 hours and parade in the streets until they arrive in the main plaza of town. It's a spectacular spectacle that captures the imagination and soul leaving a lasting impression for life.[41]

The Lesson: Be Bold & Unforgettable

Propelling a brand forward takes more than tactical knowledge and creativity. In today's competitive landscape, a brand must stand out and grab attention. It is not enough to simply get attention though. One must deliver rich meaning and ensure that the time spent with the brand has a lasting impact.

Getting attention is rather easy. Just be loud and audacious, and someone will look. The question is what do you do with that attention once you have it. And that's where a full understanding of a brand is profound and required. Brands must reward people for their time through entertainment, knowledge, or another benefit beyond financial and utilitarian.

Just as the toritos in this bull story have purpose, a name, and a unique look, so must all brand communications and marketing. Yes, the fireworks will get attention, but what will people be looking at when they turn their heads? Will it be a dumpster fire or a beautiful torito in amazing pyrotechnica splendor that leaves the viewer in a state of awe and wonder?

---

[41] The source of this story was "National Pyrotechnic Festival," Wikipedia, last modified October, 3, 2020, https://en.wikipedia.org/w/index.php?title=National_Pyrotechnic_Festival&oldid=981575825.

Too often brands do a great job of getting attention but deliver a message that's self-serving and forgettable. While I'm sure some people are happy you are offering that steep discount, there exists a bigger question around why one should care. And that's the big question that must be answered with every messaging moment: So what? Why should I care?

The Pamplonada isn't just a means to light off some pyrotechnics. Each torito has a story. Each one is crafted by people as an expression of their passion. Each one is fantastic and memorable. The same goes for a brand. Each moment must be an expression of the brand's purpose. Each moment should tell more of the story and be worth the time invested by the Patron. When done correctly, it becomes less of an advertisement and more of a fiery display of awesome, unforgettable messaging.

The Thing about Marketing

The thing about marketing is that it's a huge topic and discipline with many parts. There is no way we can cover the details and nuances of effective marketing in one book, let alone one chapter of that book. Many articles, books, courses, videos, and speaking engagements have been created to build upon marketing knowledge and deliver expert insights, and even they don't come close to telling the full story. Marketing is a vast wonderland, and borders have yet to be found. But fret not!

I do intend to give a baseline understanding of the mechanics of propelling your brand forward through effective marketing. This will get the ball rolling for you. My hope is that it also sparks a desire to learn more and continue your educational journey. With a baseline understanding, you can at least start to ideate and develop an approach to remarkable marketing that grabs attention.

No matter how far we come with technology, some tenets remain the same. Marketing requires reach and frequency to be effective. Humans must encounter messaging at least seven times before taking action,[42] and marketing isn't a switch that you can simply turn on and see results. Despite new technologies and media, these truisms only become reinforced, so it's best to understand them, believe them, and leverage them to your advantage.

Reach & Frequency

Reach and frequency have been critical cogs in the marketing strategy machine for a very long time. Reach covers the number of individuals that will see a message and creative. Frequency is how many times they'll see it. Historically, the theory of reach and frequency has been to hit as many people as possible as many times as possible. Maximizing both would see results. However, things have shifted a little bit.

No longer do we have to "spray and pray" with messaging, meaning we don't have to blindly maximize reach and frequency in the traditional sense. Today we have the ability to be more targeted by important segmentation opportunities like demographic and geographic parameters. This changes the definition of "maximizing" a little bit. In today's technological reality, maximizing reach and frequency is about simultaneously optimizing the messaging to the audience you wish to reach.

---

[42] "The Rule of Seven," TutorialsPoint, accessed April 15, 2021, https://www.tutorialspoint.com/management_concepts/the_rule_of_seven.htm.

7. Propelling Brands Ahead of the Herd

Yes, making sure that the audience sees and absorbs the brand's messaging as many times as possible is still vitally important, but making sure it's the right audience is now more possible than ever.

The Rule of Seven

While it may not be scientifically accurate, the basic reason for the rule remains the same. People do not react based on one interaction with a brand message.[43] Instead, it's the culmination of consistent messages across channels that wins the day.

A "channel" is defined as a media outlet that delivers messaging and information to people. It can be Instagram or your local newspaper. Even word of mouth could be considered a channel. A brand's marketing messaging and creative are delivered through multiple channels, multiple times.

A person does not need to encounter a brand's messaging seven times on one channel. In fact, that may be overkill and could be counterintuitive to the goals of the program. Instead, it's the culmination of all channels and the messaging through said channels that create the rule of seven. Clear as mud, right? Let me explain.

On any given day, a person encounters countless messages across countless channels. They scroll through social media, drive on highways littered with billboards, listen to radio, receive emails and text messages, speak with colleagues, and so on. Even walking down the street, they are encountered with advertisements for all things imaginable. Finding seven ways to present a brand's message is

---

[43] Ibid.

actually pretty simple when you think about how much advertising has been injected into our everyday lives.

Marketing Takes Momentum

One of the biggest misconceptions about effective marketing and advertising is that it's something one can just start and immediately see results. While it's true that results will come through nearly immediately, those results pale in comparison to what a marketing program can and will produce over time as it gains momentum. Momentum is very much the name of the game.

Marketing isn't a switch that can be turned on. It's more of a freight train. It takes a bit of time to get up to speed, but once up to speed, it can plow through just about any obstacle. Great marketing can help reduce negative effects from multiple influences like a stunted economy or natural disasters. It reduces long-term negative impacts and maximizes opportunities.

While it may take some time to slow down after ending marketing efforts, the result is the same. It will slow down and results will see a downturn. Getting started back up again takes time. It is my advice to start marketing, never stop marketing, and when times get tough, double-down on marketing no matter how hard that may be. There is nothing worse than encountering a leader who realized the need for marketing too late to prevent disaster.

There Is no Magic Bullet

Humanity's desire to find quick fixes and tricks of the trade are inherent. I mean, who doesn't want to get to the top with less effort? However, that thinking is wrought with misaligned expectations and a self-fulfilling prophecy of failure. When it comes to marketing, there is no magic bullet. There exists no end-all, be-all marketing tactic that's proven to get results. If there were such a tactic, everyone would be using it, and only it, for their marketing efforts.

You're going to have to come to grips with the fact that marketing is more than parlor tricks and ploys. One cannot trick their way into loyalty, and as time marches on, it becomes even more difficult to trick someone into a simple purchase. That's why aggressive deals often fall short of expectations.

To make matters worse, attention spans have deteriorated and continue to decrease, meaning a Patron's focus is all over the map and unbelievably difficult to grab for even a split second. Back in the heyday of advertising, the rule of thumb for a billboard was that you had three seconds to grab attention and deliver the message. In today's reality, three seconds would be a blessing. Instead, people are hammering themselves with hundreds of micro-moments in the forms of social media feeds. They're forced into pre-roll and interstitial advertisements on video platforms. And everywhere they turn, they're hit with another marketing message. Suffice to say, people have gotten really great at parsing information and messages to extract only the things they really want.

As a result, the effectiveness of old-school marketing thinking is pretty much zero. Gone are the days where a Superbowl advertisement could change the game for a company, or one ad could move the proverbial needle. No, instead of searching for that magic bullet, brands must embrace a new way of thinking of the marketing world. It's an ecosystem.

Ecosystems are organisms (plants, animals, microbes) that are interconnected with each other and their environment. In the marketing sense, an ecosystem is a collection of interconnected media channels and their various levels of relationships that drive towards common goals or conversions. In short, it's about the entire suite of marketing channels and opportunities and not one in particular. (We'll dig more into the ecosystem in the next section.)

Evaluating marketing tactics and channels on an individual basis can be detrimental to success. This approach puts way too much pressure on a singular channel—more than can ever be achieved. This is because the power of each marketing channel rests in the influences from other channels. When one evaluates a channel by itself, it's easy to cast doubt or label it a waste of time. Before you know it, there is a misconception that none of the channels work, and marketing is a waste of time altogether.

This pathway and thinking lead to what I call a "No Take, Only Throw" mentality. This is derived from an image of a golden retriever with a ball in its mouth. The caption reads, "no take, only throw" implying the common interaction with a dog in the game of fetch. For those that don't know, a lot of times the dog doesn't want to let go of the ball. But they do want you to throw it. It's funny in this scenario, but infuriating in the business world.

A "No Take, Only Throw" mentality is extremely frustrating inside and outside an organization. It's marked by a disbelief in marketing but a demand to see results. Budgets are cut to razor-thin levels, but astronomical results are demanded. It's a lose-lose situation but one I've encountered many times.

While consulting with a small multi-unit franchised brand, I encountered a group of people who had been beaten down by poor marketing consultants and advisors. Whether it was the advertising agency who sold in tons of ad spend on sports sponsorships or the tenacious elder statesman who clung to *The Tipping Point* book and all of its information as law of the land, this company had been through a ringer.

When I stood in front of the franchisees for the first time, I might as well have lit myself on fire. The skepticism was thick, and their apprehensions about working with another "marketing guy" were made very clear. Luckily I was raised in the Northeast United States where people stab you in the front. I'm used to being jawed out, so I was no worse for the wear. I was, however, concerned about the future of the relationship and whether or not we could realize success together. And we really hadn't even started yet!

I resolved to persevere, and so did the leadership despite the palpable skepticism and the reality that some folks may have been rooting for failure. It's amazing what some people will do to feel that they were right about something. It's like rooting for the pilot to crash the plane you're in because you told everyone he was a bad pilot.

A year after we took the reins at this company, the tone of the franchisees was completely different. Through consistent communication around what we were doing, why we were doing it, and what the results were, we were able to foster trust in Vigor and in marketing as a whole. We not only showed the good results but also the bad. We explained what we were seeing and why we were seeing it. We were unafraid to "take it on the chin" if someone challenged the thinking or strategy. We explained in detail so that leadership could understand the nuances.

If someone looked at the data from a channel-by-channel approach, they would have easily marked some channels as a waste of investment. For instance, YouTube was part of our strategy. It generated very few conversions in the form of click-throughs. However, the ads on that channel received millions of views. By introducing the ecosystem concept in conjunction with marketing theories, the franchise group was able to understand that even though this channel didn't drive conversions, it did fuel the means to that end. A "magic bullet" mentality would have stripped this out immediately.

Magic-bullet thinking is dangerous and simply myopic. It is my suggestion to destroy that thinking within yourself, your team, and your organization as a whole. Seek to foster understanding in the ecosystem theory throughout your organization, and you'll develop a sense of concerted effort behind the marketing initiatives as well as belief in the possibilities. Both are positive forces that can drive successful marketing.

The Marketing Ecosystem in Action

A brand's marketing ecosystem consists of four components: Drivers, Destinations, Amplifiers, and Conversions. When presented visually, it showcases the interconnectedness of each media channel along with the core purpose of that channel (See figure 05.) Some ecosystems are complex with many different channels. Others may be more basic, especially the cases where a brand is just starting out.

Every marketing media channel has a place in the ecosystem, and many may hold multiple places. For instance, a social media channel

fig. 05

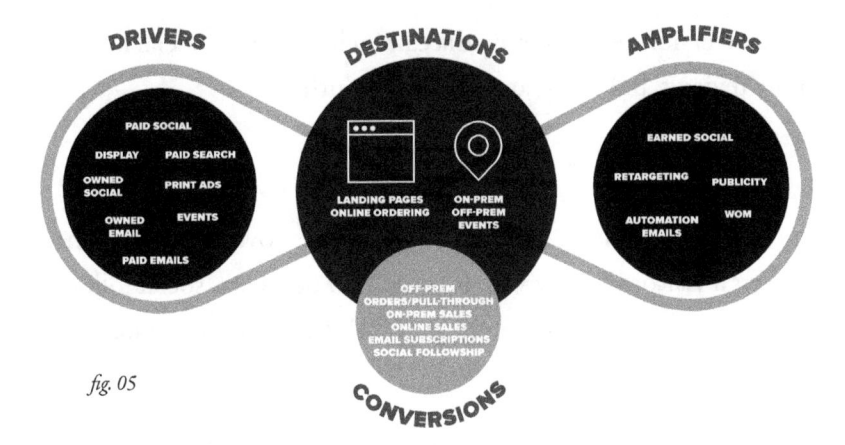

DRIVERS — PAID SOCIAL, DISPLAY, PAID SEARCH, OWNED SOCIAL, PRINT ADS, OWNED EMAIL, EVENTS, PAID EMAILS

DESTINATIONS — LANDING PAGES, ONLINE ORDERING, ON-PREM, OFF-PREM EVENTS

AMPLIFIERS — EARNED SOCIAL, RETARGETING, PUBLICITY, AUTOMATION EMAILS, WOM

CONVERSIONS — OFF-PREM ORDERS/PULL-THROUGH, ON-PREM SALES, ONLINE SALES, EMAIL SUBSCRIPTIONS, SOCIAL FOLLOWSHIP

may be a driver, a destination, and an amplifier depending on the ecosystem and the brand's needs.

Drivers

Media channels that push messages into the Patron's view and drive them towards a destination are considered Drivers. In this category could be owned and paid social media, email marketing, traditional paid advertising, on-premise marketing collateral, and various other media.

Destinations

Quite obviously, these are the places you want Patrons to go. The most obvious one is a location for your restaurant, but don't leave it at that. Destinations could include an event, social media channel, landing pages on your website, and online ordering or reservations systems.

Amplifiers

This category covers the media channels where messages get amplified either from Drivers or Destinations, pre-conversion and post-conversion. Amplifier media can include earned social media, online reviews, publicity, and word of mouth.

Conversions

This is where the magic happens. Conversions cover any action that converts a visitor in some way. It could be a purchase, social follow or engagement, email list signup, and various other measurable metrics.

The role of visualizing the ecosystem is to keep the relationships between channels clear and present. This ensures that the team, whether it's your internal team or an agency partner, understands the suite of media for each initiative and the brand as a whole. The visual nature of the ecosystem empowers teams to think beyond one channel at a time to consider the full journey and possibilities of every effort. The result is a more holistic approach to every marketing initiative for the brand.

From this ecosystem, a quicker path to plotting out the Patron's journey from beginning to end emerges. A team can identify the areas that will drive that patron to a destination, understand the role that destination plays in driving conversion, and how messages can be amplified after the fact.

If you're small and starting out, your brand's ecosystem may not be very complex. In fact, I'd advise that you keep things simple so you can execute and activate without getting overwhelmed. The opportunities for expanding the ecosystem are seemingly endless, but that doesn't mean you must take advantage of every single one of them. Keep it simple, and you'll be able to activate. Make it complex, and the chances of it falling apart are exponentially greater.

Understanding the Patron Journey

Patrons are on a journey with every brand in their world. At the very beginning of that journey, the Patron is in a state of being unaware and disinterested in the brand. Put bluntly: They don't know about you, and they don't care. The goal of marketing is to guide Patrons from that beginning to various stops along the way (figure 06). Each stop is a step closer to the golden moment of brand advocacy.

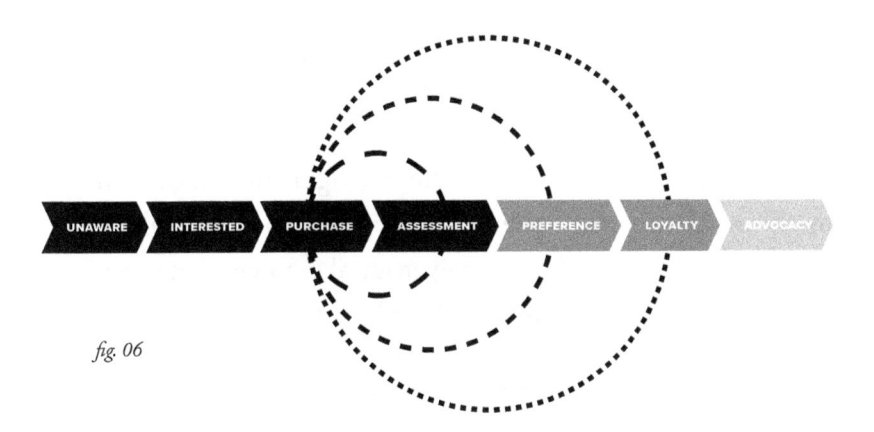

fig. 06

UNAWARE › INTERESTED › PURCHASE › ASSESSMENT › PREFERENCE › LOYALTY › ADVOCACY

Brand advocacy is a level of affinity that not every Patron will realize with your brand. A select percentage will make it to that level, but others will stall out somewhere earlier in the journey. That's okay because the few who do realize advocacy are invaluable assets to the brand. They are least likely to jump ship when a new shiny brand presents itself. They stay loyal during tough times, and they spend more when times are good.

While every Patron is different, their journey follows a consistent pattern. They start in the beginning state of unawareness and disinterest, and through interactions with the brand, they move forward to a state of varying degrees of awareness. As they encounter the brand they warm up to it and their interest increases. During this phase they start digging into the brand, conducting what amounts to research, even if they don't consider it research.

When a Patron's interest grows, they look to the brand's channels to answer questions they may have. Destinations like websites and social media pages become an area of interest. Patrons will dig into the social feed and brand's website to build their understanding of the brand and fuel their perceptions of how the brand is positioned. They're looking to answer the questions "Is this brand for me? Does it align with my values and optics?"

With enough digging and consistent messaging from the brand's marketing Drivers, the Patron's interest peaks, and they make the decision to purchase. This is a truly magical moment that ropes in the full team. This is where the rubber hits the road.

A Patron's experience during the purchase process, whether it's digital or physical, must be seamlessly exemplary of the brand. It must deliver on all the promises made in marketing and communications and then some. After all, meeting expectations isn't remarkable. Exceeding them is and that's the goal. When a Patron's expectations of a brand experience are exceeding, they are more likely to come back. Therefore, operations must be fantastic. Service must be next level. Order accuracy must be on point. And, metaphorically speaking, all the stars must align.

During and after the purchase moment, Patrons are evaluating the experience. They look to confirm their expectations. They look for places where the brand didn't live up to its promises. They make note of what they want to try next time around. This evaluation process may happen subliminally, but it's the deciding factor in

7. Propelling Brands Ahead of the Herd

whether or not the Patron will continue down the path with your brand.

If the brand experience under-delivered or displayed anything that was antithetical to what was promised in marketing and communications, the chances of a second purchase are drastically reduced. And it doesn't take a massive mistake or misalignment in expectations for a Patron to throw in the towel. After all, there are plenty of fish in the sea, and in this case, the "fish" are other restaurants with great food and experiences.

Let's say you aced the purchase moment, and the Patron is elated. #HighFive. Their journey with your brand is far from over and advocacy is not assured. At this moment your relationship with the Patron enters into a cyclical system of evaluation and assessment. They choose to come back and experience the brand again and again becoming a repeat Patron. During each of those moments, they're evaluating and building their level of loyalty to the brand.

With enough consistently elating experiences with the brand, a Patron may develop Preference. This is different from loyalty, but it is still a powerful state for a brand to realize with a Patron. Preference is marked by a consistent cadence of dining moments and an increase in check average. When a Patron prefers a restaurant over others, they're more likely to suggest it to a group of friends or family. They'll go out of their way to drive to the restaurant, even if it's slightly inconvenient.

Many Patrons will stay in a state of Preference and never move forward in the journey, but a percentage will continue on their path. The next state in the journey is loyalty, and this is a big one. Loyal Patrons are connected to the brand across various channels including social media, email marketing, and an app if one is available. They love the brand, and they tell their friends and family about it. Their dining moments with the brand may be multiple times a week as opposed to a few times per month.

Loyal Patrons want to be rewarded for their loyalty. They look to collect points with their purchases and want to be invited into the fold with exclusive offers. Those offers do not have to be discount-driven. Instead, they should be value-adding. Maybe it's an exclusive event where the chef introduces them to potential new dishes on the menu, or maybe it's early access to a limited-time offer. Maybe it's both. There is no wrong answer with how much a brand should do for its loyal Patrons, yet some brands only tick the boxes.

There is nothing worse than a brand that spends a large part of its budget attempting to get new Patrons and only servicing those who have bought in on the Preference and Loyalty states. From the Patron perspective, it's infuriating and a surefire way to reduce their level of engagement if left unaddressed. A good example of this outside of the hospitality industry is with cable companies.

Cable companies drop huge discounts and offers with the goal of attracting new customers. Once a customer buys-in, they do very little to keep them. The rates go up, and the perks expire, and the customer is left with a lackluster experience. The only thing that keeps them with the company's services is habit or the lack of motivation to make a change. Both motivations are usually overcome with another discount until a better option presents itself. Discounting as an approach to customer retention commoditizes the brand over time, and being a commodity is a terrible business model for a restaurant.

The loyalty state is not the final, ultimate state for a Patron and a brand. The final state for a Patron to realize is advocacy. When a Patron is an advocate for the brand, they'll do anything to drive it ahead. They not only suggest it to their friends, they emphatically tout it. They'll support the business through good times and bad. They'll wear your brand's t-shirt because they love it (so long as it's an awesome shirt.)

You may laugh, but the wearing of a brand's merchandise is a huge indicator of Loyalty and Advocacy. It's a big indicator that the brand has reached lifestyle level. Lifestyle brands operate on another level beyond commodity. When someone chooses to adorn a brand on their person, they are true advocates.

Advocacy is the golden moment in the relationship between a brand and its Patron. While this is the "end" of the journey visually, it's not necessarily the end. It's hard to lose a brand advocate, but it can be done. If a brand starts to overpromise and underdeliver, the Patron will start to become jaded. If the brand shifts any part of their concept without communications, the Patron may feel left out. All of these shifts and more can cause a Patron to lose interest in a brand.

Brand advocates should be cherished and fostered. There is no easy or quick path to that level or any level in the journey beyond the one that's next. It takes consistent messaging across the ecosystem and a dedication to over-delivering at every opportunity. Understanding the Patron's journey and how marketing ushers them ahead is critical in every successful marketing endeavor and charging the brand forward.

Evergreen and Campaign Marketing

Marketing efforts come in two core forms: Evergreen and Campaigns. Both are important to activate and maintain, but they are unique and have different agendas. Understanding the difference will help you and your team realize a best-in-class marketing program.

Evergreen marketing is defined as topics and creative that are perennial or relevant at all times of the year—no matter what's happening or what's new, Evergreen campaigns maintain their relevance. They can include topics such as gift card sales, online ordering, standard menu items, recruiting, and franchise sales, if applicable. These topics never lose relevance and should serve as the basis for Evergreen marketing efforts.

Campaign-based marketing and advertising are more ephemeral. They have a clear beginning and a clear end with clear objectives to hit in that period of time. Campaign-based marketing and advertising can include limited-time offers, new product promotions, new restaurant openings, and events.

While these two categories of marketing are different, they don't represent an either/or option. Both should be activated to effectively market a brand and its offering. Evergreen initiatives supply a never-ending, ongoing effort that builds a foundation for brand growth and successful marketing campaigns. Marketing campaigns give flavor and life to brand communications, causing surges in traffic and sales while keeping things from getting stale. In short, campaigns give people a reason to pay attention by breaking up the monotony of Evergreen messaging.

In my experience, I have found that strong efforts include a consistent evergreen foundation that includes paid search engine marketing, covering product-based keywords, geographic keywords, and local search optimizations. In addition to the paid search, using display banner advertising and paid social media advertising helps create an effective marketing foundation.

From that basis, campaigns can be launched that accentuate the brand and highlight the offering. Campaigns can really flex the power of marketing channels by creating a unique ecosystem that maximize reach, frequency, and Patron engagement. This results in optimal traction from campaign to campaign.

A good example of a successful mix of evergreen and campaign-based marketing is in the work my agency created for the brand Erik's DeliCafé. Investing a notably small budget in both evergreen and campaign marketing initiatives, we were able to see same-store sales lift month-to-month and year over year. Here's how that played out.

We created multiple evergreen efforts using the Google Search network spanning both search, local listing management, and display advertising. We combined standard search marketing using keywords and geo-targeting, and combined it with re-targeting efforts, which sought to attract Patrons who had interacted with the brand on one of the tracked channels (e.g., website, social.) This created a basis for growth and gave the team enough room to optimize the efforts month-to-month.

With that foundation, we launched a number of limited-time offers on a campaign basis throughout the year. Each one accentuated the menu item and gave it more character than ever before. We quite literally made characters out of the food! These campaigns also followed a formula that collectively built brand awareness and triggered high recall.

Despite having a very small budget, we were able to move the needle across the brand due to the combined efforts of evergreen and campaign-based marketing. One without the other would have not seen as much success in my opinion because of their symbiotic relationship. Combined with stellar creative that charged beyond the basic, the collective effort was one of the most successful for the brand.

The 3 Components of Remarkable Creative

Having reach and frequency may be the basis for strong marketing efforts, but without remarkable creative it will only go so far. But what makes creative remarkable? What makes one campaign successful and another a failure? In my career I've found that most successful marketing and advertising endeavors have three components: the creative grabs attention, it makes it worth paying attention to, and it is unique enough to remember.

Maybe that seems obvious to you, or maybe it seems relatively easy to accomplish. However, if you pay attention, you'll realize that not many marketing and advertising moments connect all three. Instead, they may have that attention-grabbing factor but fail to deliver on attention worthiness and memorability. Without the combination of all three, the investment in media is not reaching its full potential for return.

Without remarkable creative, marketing efforts fall flat. You've seen "flat ads" before. Just think of every single television spot for Longhorn Steakhouse. It features footage of a sizzling steak. You probably cannot recall what the voiceover said because it was so unremarkable. Furthermore, you wouldn't know what restaurant the ad was marketing if it weren't for a logo slapped somewhere.

By now, I truly hope you have the deep understanding that we're not in the business of marketing food. So creative that solely focuses on the food will always be ignorable. Yet, advertisers, marketers, and brands will still demand the "crave" shots, just like beer brands must do the pour. It's boring, trite, and forgettable.

The formula for successful, remarkable creative rests on the ability to tap into the Patron's behavioral drivers and not the baseline need of sustenance and hunger-sating. Good thing we spent some time diving into archetypes earlier in this book as those are the roots of behavioral shifts. By understanding the Patron's realities, one can craft messaging and creative that taps their desired state, making creative operate on a visceral level.

These three components of remarkable creative can leverage the power of behavioral drivers to create messaging that connects. Let's look at them in greater detail so that you can start evaluating your current marketing and queue up better creative moving forward.

Make it Noticeable

Anyone can get attention. Strip naked and run down the street, and you'll be sure to have everyone's undivided attention, even if for only a moment. The question is, is that attention relevant to your brand? And is it the right kind of attention? Probably not.

Getting attention in the context of a brand takes more than parlor tricks and antics. A brand must get noticed in a way that makes sense for the brand's values and personality. It must align with its strategy. That narrows the field of play quite a bit.

The right way to get noticed is by doing things that other brands aren't doing. Kill the crave shots, hyper-focus on the product, and create something unexpected—something refreshing to the people who are bombarded by advertising every second of every day.

Make it Worthwhile

Once you have someone's attention, don't abuse it with a hard-sell message akin to a used car salesman. People hate to be sold to, but they love to buy. In order to get them to buy, you have to make it worth the person's time. They should walk away feeling like their time was well-spent rather than perceiving the ad as an intrusion into their day.

You have to ensure that the content you deliver is engaging, interesting, and worth their time. In order to do that, you have to put their needs and realities first, not your own. People want to feel something. They want to laugh, cry, or be challenged. They engage with content that delivers on those emotions and are more likely to share it.

Make it Memorable

Just because something got your attention and delivered some value doesn't mean it'll be remembered. Memorability happens when you've profoundly tapped an emotion and filled a need within the Patron. That's a complex ask, but when accomplished, it has amazing results.

7. Propelling Brands Ahead of the Herd

To compound the complexity, a remarkable advertisement isn't only memorable on its own but also memorable in its tie to the brand. There's nothing worse than a memorable ad whose brand association is completely lost.

A great example of remarkable advertising is with Arby's "We Have the Meats" campaigns from the mid-2010s. For those unfamiliar, Arby's launched a fantastic ad campaign that was built on a simple formula: white screen, focus on one menu item, and a thunderous voiceover provided by Ving Rhames.

Mr. Rhames delivered quippy sayings chock full of humor. The payoff for the viewer was humor to the point of laughing out loud from time to time. They were truly a joy to watch, and because they didn't feature meaningless buzzwords and standard-issue crave footage, they were highly memorable.

The "We Have the Meats" slogan was a brilliant departure from its predecessor, "Slicing Up Freshness." Its low-cost production allowed for many videos to be produced and media to be well invested across channels. It challenged the common formats for restaurant advertising and delivered value. A total win across the board.

Arby's has since stepped away from that creative approach and slogan. While they continue to use "We Have The Meats" as a slogan, it's delivered in a self-serving, boring way. Gone is Mr. Rhames and his beefy voice delivering humor. Instead, the brand is back to focusing on all the same things the competitors are doing: Freshness, quality, blah blah blah.

Brands have to break away and do something different to get that valuable attention. Once they have it, they must deliver selfless value to the Patron, and they better do it in a way that gets remembered not only for the creativity but for the brand, too. And while the need to evolve and change with the times is ever-present, brands need to ensure their marketing hits all three of these components for remarkability in order to stay ahead of the herd.

Social Media Isn't Advertising

Social media may be one of the most amazing innovations of our lifetime. The ability to engage and interact with people outside of the four-wall experience is fantastic. The ability to tell a brand's story over the course of time without having to pay exorbitant amounts of money in media is unprecedented. And yet, brands and marketers have found a way to exploit the platforms and take the social aspect away. Instead, many approach social as an advertising opportunity as they ram down hard-sell messaging and tactics left and right.

Social media is not advertising. It's an opportunity to engage with patrons and develop rapport. Social media empowers an ongoing conversation that should be fed with valuable, selfless content that lives the brand's values in real-time. Yet, brands continue to see it as a marketing endeavor, and they apply old-school marketing thinking to their efforts. Then, they wonder why it doesn't get traction.

I like to think of marketing, especially social media marketing, as a social gathering or party. Social media plays by the same unwritten rules as a social gathering. For instance, if you walk into a party and the first thing you say to the room is "Hey everyone, I'm really cool!" you're immediately not. And you'll have a very hard time convincing anyone otherwise. People don't tell people they're cool.

They act like it and let others say it about them.

In a social gathering, you look to build rapport. Yes, you do get opportunities to speak about yourself, but it's more about getting to know the folks with whom you speak. You look to find common ground and shared interests. You tell stories aimed at entertaining the guests, and you seek to display your personality in full view. The same goes for social media.

People scroll through social feeds to be entertained and to learn. They want content that catches their eye and delivers value to them. They also evaluate brands based on their content, looking for reasons to believe or disbelieve the brand's claims.

When a brand treats social media as an advertising platform, they become a salesperson at a party. No one invites people to parties with the intent of harassing guests. That's exactly how it feels on social media. And just like in real life, people tend to ignore and avoid salespeople.

You are probably thinking, "If I cannot sell my brand on social media, then why bother with it at all?" It's not that social media doesn't drive sales. How it drives sales is different from the traditional advertising methodology of hard sell. Social media is less forward and blatant and more alluring. It's a long-term play, not a short-term exploit. That said, social media can drive sales so long as it's done the right way.

Social media fuels believability in a brand's claims by introducing content they wouldn't find elsewhere. It's an opportunity to tell stories that bring the Patron inside the fold, thereby creating stronger connections with the brand on an emotional level. Here are some ways you can activate this for your brand:

Take them behind the scenes

When people get a peek behind the scenes, they feel a special connection to the brand. This could be a little walk through the kitchen while people are making food. It could be a candid message from the founder or leader of the brand. The behind the scenes moments make the brand real and approachable and create awesome connectivity to Patrons.

Tell them unique stories

People love stories. They engage and spark the imagination while delivering unique insights and knowledge. When stories are told well, they are sticky, and they rope people into the brand's bigger narrative. They also get retold to others, which means great stories will spark word of mouth via a "did you know that…" inquiry amongst groups of friends.

Make a human connection

Humans connect with human brands. Therefore, brands must seek to connect on a human level with real, genuine emotions. Laughter, love, mystery, intrigue, and fun are all emotions that connect with people. When a brand delivers on these emotions in a way that's driven by entertainment and storytelling, people feel a closer connection.

More than holiday hopping and food porn

For a long time, social media thrived on imagery of food, also known as "food porn," and exploiting obscure holidays like "National French Fry Day." That worked in the past, but with the mass adoption of social media, it's lost its traction. Brands have to dig deeper than basic images of food and lazy exploits of holidays. You have to find something more—something with substance that connects to the brand.

Go beyond the feed

Posting static images to a social media platform's feed is baseline. There are so many more opportunities that are getting way more traction for brands, and those opportunities should be leveraged as much as possible. Have a look at Instagram for instance. They have Stories, Live, and TV all available for brands to leverage to deliver messaging that engages guests way more than the standard feed. So think beyond that core feature of a social platform and develop new ways of connecting with guests.

Social, like all technology, is ever-changing and ever-growing. It may be tough to keep up with what's happening, but the payoffs for doing so are tremendous. People want to connect with brands on these channels so long as the brands don't abuse that connection. They don't want to be sold, and they'll reject brands that exploit the platform for that purpose. Instead, deliver entertainment and value through robust storytelling and behind-the-scenes moments, and you'll foster a fantastic relationship with followers. That relationship will blossom into measurable results in the form of sales, repeat traffic, and success overall.

Cheap Marketing Isn't Cheap

As soon as the story breaks that you're opening a restaurant, the phone calls begin pouring in from media with "the best way to market your restaurant." They come at such a great price, and you should totally try them out. All these other brands have, and they're successful! And the pitch continues.

The cost is usually approachable and sounds too good to be true. But the budget is right, and if those other brands are winning, why not? It seems like a great move, and that you can mark that marketing checkbox as "done" and move onto other pressing matters. This is a mistake.

The too-good-to-be-true marketing solutions are exactly that. They're a cheap service that begets few results except taking your money. In the short-term and long-run, they're not actually cheap at all. While they push things out into the world on behalf of your brand, they're diluting it and deteriorating the hard work you've put in to get it off the ground.

How can I make such blanket statements? Simple math. There is no feasible way a company can create custom, on-brand messaging and designs across multiple media channels for $500 a month. The only way that number works is if they're sharing assets and messaging across many clients. That means the post that just showed up on your restaurant's Instagram is probably showing up on some other brand's feed, too.

That may not be a big deal for the mom-and-pop sandwich shop on the corner, but that's not you. You're building a bullish brand that's poised to charge ahead. Cheap marketing won't do. To charge ahead, you need to be shouting your brand's message in your brand's voice from your brand's heart.

Marketing takes multiple talents from multiple individuals. It's not as simple as posting some things to social media and calling it a day. Whether that team is with an agency or inside your organization, the truth remains that it does, in fact, take a team to create and activate strategies.

Day-to-day, month-to-month, a marketing team endeavors across multiple disciplines from research and strategy through creative design and copywriting. While you may find a unicorn who can wear multiple hats, the question of their effectiveness and abilities will boil down to there only being a certain amount of time in one day. Let's boil that down a little further.

For a successful, basic marketing effort, many things need to happen. Someone needs to research competitors and monitor their actions daily, weekly, and monthly. They need to distill out the learnings and findings, then adjust the brand's strategy accordingly. The brand needs a marketing strategy across channels, and each channel has nuances and idiosyncrasies regarding what's effective and what's not. For example, what works on Instagram won't work on Twitter. Therefore, a brand needs someone who's intimately familiar with each channel's nuances and stays on top of their algorithmic shifts. As the algorithms shift, so must the strategy and activation.

Joining the effort is the need for a designer and a writer to create content. Rare is the case where someone is excellent at both with the workload required. What I mean by that is, you may find a designer who can write a cool headline, but can they write cool headlines and supporting copy, understand hashtags, and do that all at the scale of social, print, and digital media month-to-month? The answer is no.

Jumping into the mix is the need for a team member to manage the scheduling of posts and campaigns, interacting with followers, and reporting. Finally, someone needs to keep this team on task and on time. To tally it up, any successful marketing effort would have a team of no less than five people working at least 15-20% of the time on the brand's efforts. If you do some quick math, you can easily see how $500 a month doesn't cut it.

If you're a larger brand, you probably already know this as you have experience working with agencies. However, the perceptions of the amount of time endeavors take to accomplish, and the size of the team required, are usually skewed and off base. The larger the need, the larger the team and the larger your budget will need to be.

While it's important to be fiscally responsible when it comes to how you invest your marketing dollars, cheaping out has zero positive upsides. It prevents any real traction from happening and diminishes the importance of marketing. It's true that you may find an agency or freelancer who will do things on the cheap for a time, but those scenarios are quite temporary, and soon you'll be finding yourself on the hunt for another partner. Turnover is a time and money suck, even when it comes to agency partnerships.

Discounts Discount the Brand

It's not all about price. Say it with me! It's-Not-All-About-Price! So many restaurateurs think the path to increased sales or recovery from economic downturns relies on pricing. It's a red herring that causes poor decision-making when it comes to operations and marketing.

Price is only one component of the Patron's decision to buy, and it's something that's directly influenced by many other factors. Value-to-price ratios affect the Patron's perception of whether or not something is worth the cost. Essentially, answering the question of why something costs what it does changes how people perceive the price itself.

A few years back some acquaintances of mine decided to open a restaurant and bar in Decatur. When I probed them for reasons why this bar will be unique and different, I received numerous answers. One, in particular, was repeated, "We're going to have a fantastic Filet Mignon, and it's only $14!" They were convinced this was a sticking point and something that'd get the town talking.

When they zeroed in on the $14 Filet as their claim to fame, I had to challenge them. My question was simple, "Would a $500 brand new Porsche sound good to you?" They responded with a perplexed look. I went on, "It's the same Porsche as all the others, but it's only $500. Are you a little skeptical? Do you have questions?" They responded that they'd take that Porsche in a display of hubris, but deep down they knew what I was getting at.

Quite bluntly, a $14 filet mignon sucks, even if it doesn't, because the cues of quality are missing. No, not everything that's good has to be expensive, but when it comes to some things, the expectations of price must be met. A filet mignon isn't just a cut of meat. It's a statement. It should come at a price equivalent to the quality of the cut. Selling a great cut for a cheap price isn't appealing because any barriers to purchase do not involve pricing.

Rather than causing a massive flood of hungry guests, the novice restaurateurs learned a hard lesson. Discounts discount the brand, and price-based thinking is a recipe for failure. They closed their doors about three months after opening.

One of the most common forms of discounting is found with coupons. To this day, there are people who are convinced that couponing is the path to success. Heck, the pizza industry is riddled with discount-marketing as the go-to approach. Furthermore, technologies like Groupon and RetailMeNot capitalize on coupons and people who are coupon-hungry.

The issue with coupons is that it attracts a group of people who are not poised to become loyal. Their loyalty only goes as far as the discounts you're willing to offer. Once you kill the coupons, they go to the next place to get their savings. That leaves a brand with a bump in traffic but a slump in sales. Often, a brand will go right back to discounting in an effort to boost that traffic once again. But how valuable is traffic received by cutting the profitability? I say, not very valuable at all.

Some brands think that coupons are the key to getting people to try out a new brand. I've seen startup brands launch aggressive coupons in the market using that magic word, "FREE!" I recall one brand being adamant that the free french fries coupon was the key to success. #MagicBulletMyth. They printed out thousands and handed them to everyone possible. The redemption rate was abysmal, leaving them with the question of why?

My response was simple. Nobody wants free french fries because they ask themselves, "How good can free french fries really be?" This is especially true from an unknown brand. When we informally asked people, the presumption was confirmed. They saw the free french fries offer as desperate and an indicator that the fries weren't really good. Once that perception is delivered, it's really hard to overcome it.

At best, discounting via coupons will give a brand some traffic. The hope is that that traffic will eat the food they otherwise weren't willing to try, then fall madly in love with it and come back over and over, paying full price. It's a dream —a myth—it ain't real. In reality, that traffic bump is from discounters and couponers, and they go as fast as they come.

In Real Life: A Promotion Without Purpose is Nothing to Celebrate

I can have a pretty big mouth at times. When a journalist calls me for an opinion, I don't pull any punches, so long as I have data to back up those opinions. So in 2014, when I had the opportunity to speak with Alexander Kaufman of the Huffington Post regarding TGIFridays "Endless Apps" promotion, the gloves came off. (I'm not entirely sure I ever had them on.)

To bring you up to speed, in 2014, TGIFridays launched a new promotion where one could enjoy endless appetizers for only $10 per person. Quite the deal! The brand launched this promotion with a full advertising push that included the quintessential hero shots of food and sauces. Typical. Expected.

When Mr. Kaufman called for a comment, I jumped right in. "If they're just up-selling the alcohol, the promotion just looks like a ploy. They're saying, 'We'll do anything to get you into a Fridays for a meal' — it's too kitschy, too car sales-y. It's low class." I then delved deeper into why this was a bad move for a brand that had a lot of other bad moves broiling inside and out. I wasn't nice, but I wasn't lying.

Lo and behold, the president of TGIFridays at that time, Mr.

Nick Shepherd, wasn't too pleased and had his PR team reach out for some face time. I accepted the invite and booked a flight to Nashville.

As the flight was landing in Nashville, I got a sudden surge of nervousness. I knew what I had said on record wasn't what a leader wanted to hear. A mix of wonder and dread filled me up that only broke once I shook Mr. Shepherd's hand. He greeted me with a smile, as he was backed by his trusted publicist who followed suit.

Over the next few hours, Nick unraveled how things were changing at Fridays. He delivered, with great pride, the operational eurekas he had experienced, and how they lead to massive shifts in both the back of house and front.

He rediscovered the bar's role as the energetic epicenter of the brand. Fridays had stepped away from being bar-centric over the years and, in doing so, lost the magic. More magic was lost when the operations team systematically moved away from scratch kitchens with recipes to highly consistent, time-optimized food preparation standards that put the brand around the same level of quality as prison food. Anything to save time and money while uplifting consistency.

He and I discussed menu theory and how unprofitable and unpopular menu items can guide perceptions of the surrounding elements—an associative psychological phenomenon that takes some guts to employ. Nick pointed out how the Ahi Tuna Nachos did just that and unfurled some numbers to back it.

These realizations came to him in different ways. A mix of structured analysis and research with keen observations combined to create these critical insights that lead the charge in a reclamation of Fridays' magic. His approach was to not rely on his gut or instincts solely, but to listen, learn, and activate strategies for operations, not only from a budgetary and KPIs standpoint but also from a culture-shifting necessity.

I was impressed. Learning about these insights and the measures being undertaken to get the brand back on track was exhilarating. Yet, the campaign for Endless Appetizers continued to suck. That campaign did absolutely nothing to shift perceptions of Fridays. It only reinforced the perception that Fridays was a low-cost, corporate restaurant where mediocre food at cheap prices reigned supreme.

TGIFridays had a story to tell. I knew that because I spent two hours with Nick Shepherd learning about it. But that story wasn't getting out there. It wasn't being told, and therefore, it wasn't known to the public. Without the knowledge I now had, any advertising would be flat and forgettable. And that's exactly what Endless Appetizers was, even after they made it a permanent offering in a last-ditch effort of desperation.

8. Evolving Brands

Bull Story: The Clever Bull

The Story

There once was a bull wandering through a forest. He came upon a cave near a big pond surrounded by lush, green grass. "This is an ideal place for me to settle down," the bull thought. So, he made the cave his home. The bull spent his time grazing in the meadows, becoming quite healthy and happy living in that cave.

One day, the bull was resting outside his cave house when a lion approached. "Aha! A bull! He is so healthy," thought the majestic lion, licking his lips in anticipation. The bull noticed the lion and sensed danger. "I must be on my guard now," the bull decided, as he hatched a plan.

When the lion came close, the clever bull looked into the cave and called out, "Darling, do not cook anything for dinner. I have just spotted a lion. I am waiting for it to come near." When the lion heard this, he turned and ran for his life.

A jackal saw the lion fleeing and asked, "Why are you running, Mr.

Lion?" The lion told him all that had happened. "The bull has made a fool out of you," replied the jackal. "Come with me. Together we can feast on the bull." But the lion was too scared to believe the jackal.

The jackal understood why the lion hesitated. "Alright then! Tie your tail with mine and let me lead you to the cave of the bull. In case the bull attacks, then I will be the one who will get caught first," the jackal said. The lion agreed to the plan, so they tied their tails together and set off for the bull's cave.

When the bull saw the lion coming with the jackal, he thought, "I am sure that cunning jackal knows I fooled the lion." Without panicking, the bull cried out to the jackal, "I had asked you to bring me two lions. Do you want me to keep my children hungry?"

The lion was fooled again and terrified that he had been double-crossed. He ran as fast as he could while dragging the jackal with him over stones and thorns. The clever bull outwitted his enemies, never saw them again, and lived a peaceful life in his happy cave home.[44]

The Lesson: Evolve with Purpose

A set it and forget it mentality to branding and marketing strategy can be an easy trap to fall into. Hard work is put into establishing a brand or campaign, results roll in, and it's presumed that it will work again and again. And it very well may for a time, but as time

---

[44] This story, one of the *Hitopadesha* tales, was retrieved from this website: "The Clever Bull," Telegraph, accessed April 16, 2021, https://telegra.ph/The-Clever-Bull-03-05#:~:text=Both%20the%20lion%20and%20the%20jackal%20went%20near,dragging%20the%20jackal%20with%20him%20over%20stones%20.

goes on the same strategies lose their effectiveness and marketers are faced with a renewed challenge.

When strategies are activated and never challenged, the "lion" stalks back into the picture. It could take the form of aggressive competition or consumer fatigue. It could be any number of threats restaurants face day-to-day. Sales start slipping, and before you know it, the "lion" is no longer a possibility, he's a harsh reality. Often, it's too late to shift, and a brand is rendered irrelevant with a big uphill battle ahead of it.

No matter how or when a "lion" approaches, it can be fought off and kept away with a constant dedication to evolving existing strategies and embracing innovation. In this day and age, brands must be truly innovative to keep from being eaten up by hungry lions.

What worked five years ago, or even last year, won't work now. People change. Markets shift. The landscape evolves. Your brand and marketing tactics have to do the same. At the time of this writing, the world had just gone through a violent shift due to the effects of the global pandemic. Brands that embraced the new realities and pivoted are the ones that are thriving. Brands that did not have either closed or are on the brink. The lion never sleeps.

Brands are living things in many ways, and like all living things, they age and grow. During their growth, they accumulate positive and negative elements. And before one realizes, the brand's offering to the world becomes muddied and unclear.

Additionally, the world around brands changes both slowly and rapidly. Consumer behaviors and drivers alter and shift with the times and in reaction to their own realities. New technologies drive new opportunities, and consumers adopt new behaviors. Suffice to say, who we are as humans today is not who we were yesterday and certainly not who we'll be tomorrow.

Despite these realities, many brands stick to their guns and stick to what has worked. There is comfort in the tried and true.But the tried and true may become tired and false if one is not careful and in tune with what's happening. For this very reason, evolution is a necessity that must be considered from the very beginnings of a brand's existence. If the brand already exists, then there is no time like the present to plan for the future.

How will the brand maintain its unique position and ownership over key brand attributes? How will the brand's personality evolve to maintain equity built, while maximizing the potential to attract new generations? How will the brand get stronger and continue its trajectory ahead? These questions aren't mere speculation for the sake of it. They must be answered early on, so the brand can grow and scale with confidence while continuing to thrive.

In this section, we'll cover the differences between brand evolution and rebranding and go into how to identify the gaps between the current state of the brand and the desired state. Evolving brands is not an easy task, but with the right thinking and knowledge, you can successfully evolve any brand ahead to ensure no lions or hyenas attack.

The Difference between Rebranding and Brand Evolution

There exists a clear difference between rebranding and brand evolution, yet many marketers and designers get it wrong. Rebranding a company involves a full reboot from inside out and top-down. It's a revolution. In comparison, a brand evolution seeks to reinforce the areas of the brand that are unique and strong by injecting new energy and visuals that accentuate the brand. Put simply, a brand evolution pushes the current brand forward, and a rebranding starts from square one.

When presented with a brand that's stunted in growth, leaders are essentially at a crossroads. Do you rebrand the concept into something completely new, or do you find a way to reclaim relevance by evolving the existing brand? The answer is different for every situation, but there are some guidelines to help decide what's right.

There are instances where a rebrand is the right choice for growth. They usually involve scenarios where elements of the company have drastically shifted, or events have taken place that are irreversible. Here are a few of these instances::

Change in offering. When a restaurant finds itself with a notable shift in cuisine, it may need to be rethought and reapproached completely. For instance, if the restaurant had been known for hamburgers in a full-service setting, but now it's going to offer sandwiches and salads in a quick-service model, it most likely needs a completely new brand. Whether it's a pivot in cuisine, service model, or both, evolving the brand isn't going to cut it.

Shift in Patron focus. If a brand seeks to attract new customers, a rebrand may be necessary. When a brand has been designed a certain way for a clear group of people, it's very difficult to shift to focus on a different group altogether. Chances are, the brand's visual identity is associated too much with the original Patron group, so completely redesigning the look based on the new strategy is the right path ahead.

Insolvency. If a restaurant finds itself insolvent, it's a pretty horrible moment. Failure isn't pretty. When this happens, it's usually best to not try and resurrect the brand. Failure has a way of sticking to a brand name, and it's a hard stigma to shed. Best to leave sleeping dogs lie.

Negative press. Sometimes publicity is not your friend. This is especially true for restaurants that have been hit with poor reviews or failed health inspections. These can be death knells for any restaurant. In some instances, the restaurant can recover. In many, it cannot.

Merger. In the case where one brand merges with another, some of the time it makes sense to create an entirely new brand from top to bottom. This is rare, but not unheard of.

While there may be more reasons for a rebrand, these are the most prevalent. If they don't apply to your scenario then chances are a brand evolution is the right call. In some ways, this may be a bigger hill to climb than a rebrand. With a rebrand, you get a clean slate and a fresh start for the most part. With an evolution, there are many more aspects to consider. It's more surgical and tedious.

It's important to weigh all the factors of each path before making the decision. Once the design is made, it's difficult to switch back without a loss of time and financial investment. Furthermore, irreversible damage can be done if you decide to backtrack after an evolved look or new brand is launched. The most damage coming from confused Patrons that may lose trust in the restaurant and company.

Identifying the Gaps between Current State and Desired State

With a brand evolution, leaders must analyze everything that's been done to date. Has the brand's purpose maintained clarity, and has it been effectively communicated? Has the visual identity shifted or maintained the same look? For how long? Is the brand's positioning in the competitive landscape clear? These are just a few high-level questions that a leader must ask when evaluating the state of a brand.

The goal of this analysis is to identify gaps between where the brand is today and where it needs to go. In order to finalize the review and identify said gaps, the brand's evolved strategy must be completed. The difference between developing an evolved brand strategy and the brand strategy process we covered in this book is found in the phrase, "brand equity."

Brand equity is defined as "the value a company gains from its name recognition when compared to a generic equivalent."[45] I think it goes deeper than that. Equity can be built in every facet of a brand experience from visual identity through cuisine. Over time, a restaurant builds equity in the areas that are truly unique to the brand.

A fantastic example of brand equity would be in the McDonald's

---

[45] Adam Hayes, "Brand Equity," Investopedia, updated February 23, 2021, https://www.investopedia.com/terms/b/brandequity.asp.

golden arches. They are noted as one of the most recognizable brand marks in the world. This didn't happen overnight. That recognition was fostered and built over time and through the consistent use of the golden arches. The result is valuable equity built in that one particular element of the brand. Additionally, McDonald's has built equity in its very well-known Big Mac® flagship hamburger. Shifting away from the Big Mac would be a terrible move for any evolutionary shift.

It's easy to identify equity with a behemoth brand like McDonald's, but the scale of that brand doesn't mean that equity cannot and is not built by smaller brands. Equity is built everywhere there are distinctive elements aligned with a brand. Identifying those elements is crucial for successful brand evolution.

What visual elements have been used consistently throughout the life of the brand?

Take stock of logos, typography, colors, imagery, and other graphic elements that comprise the brand's identity. Evaluate how much recognizability is associated with those elements. This can be done by an internal team but not without a certain amount of bias. My suggestion is to rely on fresh eyes from a principled agency team, tap experts at a research firm, or both.

Do those elements communicate the brand's adjusted strategy from personality through positioning?

Once you've identified the unique elements of the brand's identity, you must evaluate their alignment with the new, evolved strategy. Evaluate whether or not they are truly communicating the brand's strategic foundations. Note any elements that could be adjusted to communicate the strategy better. Note any elements that are no longer relevant or able to be redesigned.

What's missing from the suite of identity and marketing communications?

Using the evolved strategy as a lens, look for areas where messaging is weak or missing. Take note of those elements and earmark for reconsideration or creation. Ideate on the brand's strategy and how it's communicating to develop new ideas for communicating the brand in a way that's unique and powerful.

By working through these three questions, clear gaps between where the brand is today and where it needs to be should become apparent. Based on those gaps, you should be able to plot a course for evolving the brand's identity to be purely evocative of the new strategy. These questions will bring to light areas where the brand falls short in those communications to help you plan what exactly needs to shift in order to achieve a successful evolution.

The Hardest Thing to Do: Remove Excess

Through the brand evolution process, many facets of the brand may be identified as superfluous and no longer effective in communicating the brand. However, some of these facets may serve as sacred cows for leaders in the organization. Attempting to remove them could cause a stir at the very least.

Removing excess is extremely difficult. After all, those elements did contribute to any successes seen to date. When it comes to food, there are people who buy those items. It's all too easy to make the case that they should have a place on the menu as a result. This sentiment can be so ingrained that data won't budge the leader who believes that removing the item will cause a decline in sales. And, so, the items stay on the menu and the menu bloats.

I've seen these situations play out many times with many brands. I've seen hot dogs and pretzels on the menus of a brand that's top menu items were subs and fruit slushies. I've seen chicken wings crammed onto a menu predominantly filled with wraps and sandwiches. And I've seen a brand hold onto old-fashioned deli salads—macaroni salad, potato salad, and coleslaw—for dear life. These situations aren't moves, they're paralysis driven by fear of unknown results.

If something isn't adding to the uniqueness of the brand and its position, it is definitely taking away from it. There must be a concerted effort to realize the ideal and not capitulate or compromise. This is one of the few moments where a brand should be ideal, as there will be plenty of time for it to gather the excesses and irrelevances. It is part of the cycle.

One way to combat the aversion to removing elements of the brand that no longer fit is to ensure that all leaders are completely onboard with the strategy. That's why strategic workstreams should be collaborative. When this is accomplished, the leaders themselves may very well identify the excesses rather than reacting to someone else who has done it first. And, as we all know, many people are fully bought into ideas when they are their own.

Another approach to peeling back the grip on elements that are dangerous to brand evolution success is to open a safe dialogue about why a leader or leaders are so dedicated to refusing the shift. A process of question asking and answering, investigation, and conversation may help uncover the underlying reasons for the seemingly irrational stance. Once uncovered, together the team can collaborate on appropriate actions to take.

Maybe the food item was created by the founder's mother. Even if it's not a big seller, it could be reapproached in a more modern format. For our friends at Erik's DeliCafé, this was the case with the carrot cake. That cake was a family recipe, and it was absolutely fantastic. But it existed around no other dessert items, and it was presented as a cake that required slicing to serve, which presented another issue. Some slices were bigger than others, and customers would complain if they did not receive a slice to the size of their liking.

Through collaboration with the leadership, we were able to drive forward the idea that the carrot cake should be made into cupcakes. They're more portable, and it's easier to control consistency in size. Not only would this reduce the complaints from customers, but it'd also ensure that the brand could optimize revenue from this product. But that wasn't the only shift we suggested.

What good is one cupcake option on a menu when there are no other desserts except for prepackaged desserts created by a completely different company? We furthered our advice to include the removal of the prepackaged goods in exchange for more cupcake flavor options. This would have given more purpose behind the carrot-cake cupcakes while opening up a new line of revenue. Furthermore, it fit Erik's DeliCafé's brand purpose of having character in everything they do. Finally, it would serve up a basis for a marketing and advertising campaign sure to get traction because— who doesn't love cupcakes?!

By understanding the brand's strategic foundations, we have been able to help them evolve with much success. That evolution includes having tough discussions and decisions involving the removal of sacred cows from all facets of the business. The results are an optimal, powerful brand that's poised to charge ahead farther than ever before. While removing excess is difficult, it is a necessary endeavor if the gold standard of a brand is to be realized.

Changing with the Changing Times

Times always do change and along with it so much the brand. I write this at the risk of sounding like a broken record, but it's so critical to ongoing success. Whether you're a single-unit independent owner, or at the helm of a franchise system, the need to evolve and shift is ever-present and constant. However, it's very easy to kneejerk react to trends and find oneself in a less-than-desirable situation as a result. Therefore it's important to understand what constitutes a trend and what constitutes a permanent shift from which evolution must spark.

Trends come and go. While they may be intense for a time, their very nature is to dissipate and fall away as the next trend rises up. It's easy to mistake that intensity as an indicator of a pivotal, permanent shift in consumer behavior and buying patterns. In my time on this planet, I've witnessed countless trends. When it comes to the food space, specifically dessert occasions, we've seen the rise and fall of frozen yogurt, cupcakes, and doughnuts. In the standard food space, we've seen surges with better burgers, better pizzas, and, most recently, better chicken sandwiches.

Outside of food, there is the broader discussion of dietary trends, which have been like a rollercoaster of ups, downs, twists, turns, and loopty-loops. I've experienced the no-salt craze, the no-fat craze, the no-carbs craze, and the no-food craze in the form of juicing. We've seen high-fat diets in the form of Keto and a reclamation of prehistoric human diets in the Paleo movement. On top of this, is the rise in awareness around food allergies, where culprits like gluten and tree nuts cause a need for sensitivity from restaurant brands.

If one pays attention to these trends and takes them as indicators of pivotal permanent shifts, that person would find themselves scrambling to keep up. It could drive you mad as it's impossible to stay on top of trends. Instead, it's important to review and analyze trends to see if there is any alignment with the brand. Does the trend pose an opportunity to build belief in the brand's principles and promises, or would capitalization on that trend seem more like a cheap ploy for attention?

The answer to that question should drive what happens next for a brand. Some trends last longer than others; some come and go like flash paper. Flash paper trends should never permanently shift or evolve a brand. Instead, if a trend is in line with a brand's principles, then a limited-time offer may be a fantastic idea to capitalize on the opportunity.

If the trend has the hallmarks of becoming a permanent shift in consumer behavior, the brand may choose to create permanent offerings in response as part of its evolution practices. An example of this would be the growth in vegan and vegetarian diets that spurred on the development of meatless alternatives to the classic burger. The adoption of plant-based diets has skyrocketed year over year, and it's easy to see that it's not a passing fancy. As a result, many well-known brands have cleared a space for a permanent offering on their menu while capitalizing on the buzz that comes from such a shift.

Burger King is arguably one of the most pivotal brands to adopt the plant-based burger, and the brand was rewarded handsomely for the foresight. BK received a ton of publicity about the addition, which served as a flag in the ground for plant-based individuals. If a meat-forward brand like Burger King sees this as a legitimate consumer shift, then it most certainly must be. From Burger King's lead, other players started adopting plant-based options, and the chain reaction continues to today.

While the food offering is one source of evolutionary opportunity, it is not the only source. One of the areas where restaurants struggle is with the interior and architecture of the brand experience. Interiors and architecture are a huge investment when starting a new brand and building a new unit. At the time of the build, the restaurant is most likely on-trend, fresh, and innovative. However, that luster fades as time marches on, and if one is not careful, the space becomes dated and dull.

A restaurant interior experience is a moment of truth for patrons. It should be a gold standard brand moment from beginning to end. Therefore, it must be a purposeful goal to maintain its relevance and freshness. Despite that glaring need, many brands let their interior experiences fade.

In a lot of corporate franchised systems, agreements dictate a brand refresh at the 5-year mark, with an overhaul at the 10-15-year mark. This is a great policy when enforced, but is highly dependent on what defines "refresh" and "overhaul." Often, a "refresh" means a fresh coat of paint and some new signage. While this is an improvement, it may not be enough to keep the experience on par. It certainly isn't enough to keep the brand experience above par.

I have encountered many multi-unit brand systems. In one instance, the brand had seven concepts activated in the market. And because the system was struggling, the enforcement of standards and policies was difficult at best, impossible at worst. This left the brand in a state of misaligned experiences that resulted in patron confusion. I cannot knock the brand for the predicament in which they found themselves, but leadership had to take the need seriously and find a way to upgrade the system.

An opposite approach that I've seen is in restaurants that create a basic interior experience that's safe. These kinds of spaces are marked by having simple color schemes, basic textures and materials, and amount to a "nice" look. While this reduces the need to shift and adjust over time because basic doesn't really age, it does create a forgettable experience in that it does nothing to communicate the brand. It's simply a nice shell that could represent any brand.

Neither scenario is ideal. Instead, the suggested approach would be to create remarkable brand experiences and adjust the budgets to cover a deeper update at the 5-year mark, investing in more than just paint and signage. Financially it may be a pain point, but the results found through an aligned and modernized experience are well worth the investment.

Changing with the changing times should be a cognitive, purposeful endeavor. Successful brands know this, and they work towards staying ahead of the curve across their systems from interiors to product mix and all things in between. When taken seriously and activated with excellence, a brand can not only maintain a top position with Patrons, they can scale and grow and realize new heights.

Activate and Celebrate Internally and Externally

A brand evolution is not something that should be lightly floated out to the world. The brand has loyal patrons whose relationship with the brand could be challenged with change that isn't appropriately managed. If they see changes to a brand without context or knowledge, chances are they may get confused and see it as an inconsistency. Inconsistency deteriorates brand belief and trust.

Instead, brands that are undergoing an evolution process should plan to launch the new identity and positioning with a bang. It should be a celebration and a big moment for those inside and outside of the company. This is that one moment to shine—to go big and make a statement. My suggestion is to do it up and make a big splash.

Activating the brand internally before the rest of the world is the best move forward. If the process has been handled correctly, the internal teams are already aware of the shifts before the strategy and identity are finalized. That means the people who are most engaged with the brand, the internal teams, are, at the very least, curious about where things have netted out.

Conduct an all-hands meeting

This should be somewhere outside of the restaurant and corporate headquarters. This gets people out of the "daily grind" mentality and allows them to reset in a fresh setting. It clears their plate to focus on the topic at hand. It also establishes the sincerity and importance of the effort that will foray into more buy-in from the team.

Lead with top-level keynote

Don't launch into the new strategy and visual identity right away. Instead, the president of the company should kick off the meeting that lays the groundwork for the vision and purpose of the initiative. Answer the questions: "Why are we doing this?" and "What do we expect to happen as a result?" Answering those questions will eliminate much of the naysaying and doubt that could come from the team.

Do a big reveal

Once the leader has delivered the keynote, it's time for the big reveal. But don't simply pull a curtain and exclaim, "tada!" Instead, build up to the reveal by outlining the thinking behind the strategy. What insights were gathered from what sources? How were those insights leveraged to identify components of the strategy? How did they form into the brand's strategic platforms?

Once the leadup and story have been explained, only then, should the curtain drop on the new identity, starting with any shifts to the core logo and followed by all the details that comprise the new visual language. Take the time to point out the correlations between the findings and how they visually manifested. These stories will sink in with the team and strengthen their belief and buy-in.

Hand out swag

Definitely hand out merchandise and swag with the new brand identity in full effect. The swag shouldn't just be logos slapped on things. They should be thought through, using the brand strategy as a lens. For instance, if the brand has taken on The Explorer brand archetype and has identified adventure and the Great Unknown as part of its purpose, items like a carabiner or a Yeti thermos would make a lot of sense. But if the brand is all about that party life, then those items may not jive as much.

Answer questions

There will be questions, and how those questions are answered will be one of the first interactions with the team and the brand. Do field questions in real-time, and don't be afraid if there isn't a direct answer. Make sure the inquirer understands that that question will be looked into and a truthful response will be sent to the whole organization. Thank them for asking and engaging.

Record for those who could not attend

A huge mistake I've seen is not recording the brand-launch event. Such a big moment should be shared with the entire organization, and not everyone will be able to attend. Additionally, the content of the event is rich and detailed, making it near impossible to remember everything. A video will help jog the memory and allow people to follow up with questions after the fact. It's also great fodder for social media stories and content to start to stoke excitement with your external patrons.

Once the brand has been effectively activated inside the organization, it's time to turn the team's sights to celebrating the new look externally with the masses. The best way of doing this is by ensuring the brand is fully activated in a new location or a newly renovated location. This will give the patron's a place to fully immerse themselves in the evolved strategy and aesthetic. But the evolved space shouldn't be the beginning and the end of the reveal.

Revealing to the masses should be made into an event, just as the internal reveal was. It should be big and evocative of the brand's strategic foundations. Using the Explorer-driven brand anecdote, the reveal event could have a rock climbing wall with prizes for those who reach the top. There could be live music and giveaways. Honestly, the sky's the limit with ideas, so long as they are centered on the brand's core foundations.

I encourage you to think big when it comes to activating any brand evolution. There are no points for lightly floating a new look into the world. It's the exact opposite that will win the hearts of folks inside and outside the organization. When done right, both sets of stakeholders will have a stronger connection to where the brand is going. That kind of buy-in is invaluable.

What Does the Future Hold?

As I try to look into my crystal ball and foretell the future, I realize that I have no crystal ball and the future is truly unknown. What we do know is that things will shift and things will change. That feels no truer than in this moment as I finish writing *The Bullhearted Brand*.

We, as a world, are coming out of a pandemic that changed our way of life nearly immediately. Businesses were forced to close. People were forced to stay home. Fear of contracting the disease paralyzed the masses. Compounding the chaos was protesting and rioting in the streets. Sensationalism and activism from media sources stoked the negative in everyone, and our collection of diverse cultures seem more divided than ever.

Concurrently, the world has experienced some positives. Adoption of virtual connectivity is at an all-time high. People are using QR codes now more than ever. And there is a sense of better times ahead as we reach herd immunity and people look to reclaim their natural social selves. This positivity is a charge of goodness in the world that can spur on new, exciting experiences from all industries but especially the hospitality industry.

Food and design trends will continue on their rollercoaster ride, ebbing and flowing. What's next for them is hard to tell, but I don't believe those trends are what's truly important to consider. Instead, there are three categories of trends that could prove to be pivotal moments for restaurant brands. They should be researched and fully considered from a strategic perspective if a brand is intending to succeed for years to come.

Environmental & Social Governance (ESG)

This acronym represents the factors to be considered when evaluating the sustainability and societal impact of an organization. At the time of this writing, these factors are starting to be used to determine the future financial performance of companies. While we have not heard any financial institution make a clear commitment, there are mutterings of ESG starting to play a major role in investments in the near future.

That means that access to cash will be weighed by the company's dedication to environmental sustainability and social justice. If the company is not fully ingrained in these endeavors, it may risk denial of vital capital. Suffice it to say that environmentalism and social justice will soon shift from a unique attribute of an organization into a critical component of modern business operations. These will shift from points of differentiation to requirements of operation, and brands need to keep an eye on how this progresses.

Technological Integration

No two words could be bigger than "technological integration." Society has been steamrolling ahead on new technologies and innovations. It's near impossible to keep up. The advances we have made in the last twenty years are mind-boggling compared to the hundred years prior. But there's a problem.

To date, technological advancements have been sort of siloed in their focus. For instance, a customer relationship management (CRM) software may be focused on the features that make it competitive. While focusing on those features, they may tack on email marketing with baseline features. The issue is that feature is usually pretty basic and pales in comparison to systems built for that task.

The same goes for other technologies out there. They focus on their core but still add some tacked-on features that aren't that great. This leaves a gaping hole between systems, and to date, that hole has been loosely filled with API calls and a ton of scrambling from technology and marketing teams. The struggle is real, as they say.

Integration will be the name of the game moving forward. That will happen in a number of ways. First, mergers and acquisitions. I can easily see a world where bigger players gobble up smaller players or merge with players of similar size. After the transaction, they'll look to combine the software systems to create omnichannel, omni-feature suites.

A second way will be slower. It'll be a dedication to developing full features and functionality surrounding the "tacked on" services. This will involve tech companies securing more investment capital to build the team capable of outputting the new features.

No matter which path is taken, the same result exists. Core technologies must integrate and merge to provide a seamless experience for Patrons. Point of Sale, CRM, kiosks, and online ordering must merge in order to continue ahead. The systems that don't see this coming will either get acquired or fail out.

From a restaurant leadership perspective, companies should be pressured to work towards this gold standard. Partners must be on a path to convergence and integration if they are to be considered for partnership at all.

Automation

Automation has been a hot topic for some time now. I recall about ten years ago when the fully autonomous burger machine was being discussed. The desire to systematize basic processes is at an all-time high due to the impending shifts to minimum wage. Hikes in minimum wage will affect the bottom-line, and while some restaurants may find a way to absorb that increase, others have focused on technology and automation as a way to optimize operations.

From back of house robotics that can create food from beginning to end, to self-ordering kiosks that eliminate the need for counter help in a quick-service or fast-casual model, automation is very much the future for successful restaurant operations. This is definitely something to keep an eye on and potentially spearhead, depending on your restaurant and company's financial situation.

So what else can we expect from the future? Easy, surprises and unknowns. That's the best and worst thing about the future. No one knows what to expect, so we should all expect the unexpected. If you've followed the path outlined in this book, your brand will be well suited for whatever may come next. After all, your brand will be bullhearted and poised to continue its charge.

In Real Life: Evolving a Classic QSR with Easygoing Vibes

In the city of Tucson, Arizona, there are many hidden secrets and brands over which the citizens teem with local love. One such brand is a fast food restaurant built on the foundation of a tasty frozen drink. One part slushy, one part Italian ice, this frozen beverage and its plethora of flavors rose to the top of the list of local favorites over the course of 50 years. The brand is called eegee's and the drink is called an eegee. And when eegee's reached out to Vigor, they were faced with a challenge.

Unlike other challenges, this wasn't driven by negatives. The company was doing quite well. In fact, it was doing so well that it attracted venture capital to invest with the purpose of growth. That growth centered on expansion into the biggest city in Arizona: Phoenix.

Earlier in the company's history, leadership attempted this entry but was unsuccessful sending the brand back to Tucson with its proverbial tail tucked. This time, however, the brand was spearheaded by brilliant leadership who knew the right partners would ensure a successful endeavor. There was just one issue to overcome. The brand looked like a gas station, and the perceptions of the brand weren't very good from unaware patrons. Patrons that lived in Phoenix.

Phoenicians' low perceptions of eegee's drove leadership to engage in a rebranding initiative, and they quickly identified Vigor as their partner of choice.

Through true collaboration and teamwork, the Vigor team guided eegee's leadership and board members through a rigorous rebranding process, including in-depth research and consumer polling. The data excavated from those endeavors helped steer the ship towards a rejuvenated expression of the eegee's brand, starting with a clear view of who was most primed to love the brand and become its advocates.

We identified a youthful group of people who served not as the primary Patron, due to their prevalence in size, but their influence in new media channels that the brand had yet to successfully activate. This group of people was driven by a love of life and experiences. They sought to live life to the fullest and enjoy every moment while striving to become something more. They were unafraid to be original and counter to the prevailing cultural norms. They looked to the future while enjoying the present. We named them Sunchasers.

Eegee's was poised to connect with Sunchasers through a very clear suite of ownable, authentic personality traits, driven by a yet undefined purpose. Through our collaboration, we excavated a unique purpose for the brand: To sweeten the moment. From that epicenter, we identified an offbeat, warm, and easygoing attitude thriving throughout the organization. Although it became muddied by miscommunications and misaligned visuals, the brand was born and thrived with this underlying attitude. We had to brush off the dust and muck and bring it to full vibrant life.

The Purpose and Personality served as an initial lens to evaluate the Product and drive the Presentation layer as experienced in the visual and verbal identity and its experiential manifestation. We engaged in an analysis of the brand's financial data as it pertained to the product mix while simultaneously endeavoring to evolve the visual identity itself in a parallel path.

Through the menu data analysis, we found that the brand had some very clear winners and very clear losers. It goes without saying that the eegee beverages were the absolute stars of the menu from profitability, popularity, and perceptual drivers. French fries doused in house-made ranch dressing served as the food category leader on the menu, followed-up by a lineup of subs and grinders. Outside of these core products were a selection of misfits composed of pretzels, hot dogs, and a cup of macaroni and cheese.

We came back to the team with suggestions on removing the superfluous items while sparking them to build out the ranch-focused products, including new french fry options as well as sandwiches. While the operations and leadership team focused on those efforts, we doubled-down on the push regarding the visual and verbal identity development.

Eegee's had been through only two iterations of identity design in its lifespan. It started with simple typographic composition in a pure green color bolstered by an orange lightning bolt graphic (See figure 07.) In the 2000s, they went through a complete rebrand. A burn-down-the-house and rebuild scenario that resulted in a simple, chunky, deep-red logotype.

From there we picked up the torch (See figure 08.)

fig. 07

Fresh eyes on the identity perceived a gas station-like look and feel. It was sterile and lacked personality beyond a "drink our drink, eat our food, and get out of here" kind of vibe. Sunchasers were not going to be very interested in this look. However, we did identify some areas where the brand had built visual equity and opportunities for the brand to shine even more.

fig. 07

The Vigor team designed dozens of potential logo directions that explored various compositional solutions. After narrowing it down to three, we took the options to the Sunchasers themselves to survey their reactions. However, we did not ask them the questions you may think. Nowhere was there a question that asked if they liked the look. Nor did we ask if they thought this looked like a restaurant or frozen fruit slush brand. Instead, we asked them lifestyle questions like, "Would you wear this on a shirt?" and "Which feels the most offbeat?"

A clear winner came from the polls and was set as the final solution. It was a typographic solution that pulled some influence from the original logo with color palettes that pulled from the latest look. The only addition to the identity was a graphic element we created that represented the actual eegee beverage. We obliged leadership and cleaned up the typography on the core logo to land in a solid spot for the new eegee's identity (See figure 09.)

fig. 09

From this epicenter, we crafted a suite of elements that would evoke the easygoing, offbeat, and warm attitude. Multicolor gradients served as backgrounds and photographic filters for custom photography of food andlifestyle. Simple, offbeat line art illustrations of fruit and regional iconography added a sense of easygoing fun to the look. A selection of seals and bursts were created to be used as callouts on collateral. Finally, a suite of typography was selected to make a statement about the brand attitude and food.

These elements came to full life in the brand's core touchpoints and monthly flavor marketing materials. They also informed the development and design of a new eegee's prototype design (Figure 10) and its interior elements. We worked with the folks at Fitch, an architectural powerhouse, to design an optimized interior and exterior drive-thru that would tell the brand's story and deliver on the brand's Purpose and Personality.

Fresh one-liners and headliners were written to build the verbal identity. They were applied to collateral touchpoints inside and outside of the four-wall experience. One of the phrases stood out

fig. 10

as exemplary of the brand's personality: Take it easy, have an eegee. And this became the brand's slogan to be used not only inside each location as a wall-mounted element but also as a sendoff from team members to guests. Instead of saying "have a nice day" they were trained to say "Take it easy!"

About the time we were finishing the foundations of the brand's identity, the team had made decisions on the menu shifts. Through collaboration, we designed a completely refreshed drive-thru menu that was optimized for increasing average ticket sales metrics and pull through. Of course, the design process speculated its success, so the only option was to test it at a location where a negative impact wouldn't cause a drastic effect.

After one month of activation, the new menu's results were quite clear. A 20% uptick in sales year over year and a faster order time—both critical metrics for the drive-thru operations. And that's not the only place eegee's saw positives from the rebrand.

Patrons reacted more often on social media, showing love for the brand and its rejuvenated attitude and look. Merchandise sold out quickly every time something new was printed. Sales were significantly up even during the pandemic. And, the most notable, if you ask me, a fan of the brand got the new logo tattooed on his leg. Now that's brand advocacy.

Vigor went on to take the reins of eegee's marketing efforts, breaking sales records left and right. Through our work, we continued the march towards an easygoing, offbeat, and warm brand and built believability in the market and with our Sunchasers. The results speak for themselves in proving that this brand evolution was a huge success.

9. Charging Ahead

9. Charging Ahead

253

Bull Story: Babe the Blue Ox

The Story

We're sure you've heard the tale of Babe the Blue Ox, Paul Bunyan's trusty sidekick of epic proportions. Babe was massive in size and purpose. He helped Paul pioneer the midwest, or so the story goes.

Babe the Blue Ox was a huge asset to Paul Bunyan's logging camp. He could pull anything that had two ends, so Paul often used him to straighten out the pesky, twisted logging roads. By the time Babe had pulled the kinks out of all the roads leading to the lumber camp, there were twenty miles of extra road left flopping about with nowhere to go. So Paul rolled them up and used them to create a path into new timberland.

Paul also used Babe the Blue Ox to pull the heavy tank wagon used to coat the newly-straightened lumber roads with ice in the winter. One day, the tank sprang a leak that trickled south and became the Mississippi River. After that, Babe stuck to hauling logs. Only he hated working in the summertime, so Paul had to paint the logging roads white after the spring thaw so that Babe would keep working through the summer.

No matter what, they worked together and combined their talents like real friends and partners.

The Lesson: Find Great Partners

In today's landscape, partnerships are everything. A great partner helps brands persevere against competition, build strong followings, and jump ahead of the curve. Whether it's technology partners that help accumulate and disseminate data or creative partners like the brilliant (and humble) folks at Vigor, true partnerships propel your brand forward.

Babe set out for adventures with Paul and never wavered from his loyalty and dedication. That's exactly what brands need in a partner if they want to blaze new trails and keep people telling their tales for years to come. Yet many brands settle for partnerships that aren't up to snuff or don't fully understand the brand. That's a recipe for disaster.

Leaders of brands must be on a mission to not only identify potential partners but also evaluate them and onboard them so those partners can be powerful allies. When this goal is accomplished, the partner companies aren't there to offer products and services alone. Instead, they work in tandem to drive the brand forward in their own way—just like Babe was there to drive Paul Bunyan's work ahead.

Finding the Right Partners

The right partners are crucial to success in any endeavor, but finding them isn't as easy as asking around or looking in your local Yellow Pages. (Remember those?) The search for a partner that has the skills, experience, and expertise is hard enough. Finding one that also fits your culture makes it feel like finding a needle in a haystack. But that needle must be found.

Partners that don't align on culture and cannot deliver on what they say can set brands back money and time that can never be recouped. Yet, some companies choose to go with their gut, or simply go with what a peer suggests and not take the time and effort to evaluate the options. This is lazy and a big mistake.

I can understand the aversion to the process. It's like going on a dozen first dates with people who talk about themselves constantly. They say all the right things because they are on parade for you to evaluate. Believe me, the pressure is insane on both sides of the table. You want to make the right choice, and the success of the company is dependent on that choice. They want to win the business because the success of their company rides on that win.

The mutual pressure is why a lot of companies go with who they know or who they've heard of. There's a saying that I've heard multiple times from different parties: "nobody got fired for hiring JWT or Ogilvy." I'm sure those company names are swapped depending on the industry but the truism is the same. People know those agencies, and they have a reputation for great work.

So even if the work isn't great and the campaigns fail miserably, it can't be because of the agency selection. Alternatively, if someone takes a risk with a lesser-known agency and the campaign fails, well, the heads are on the chopping block. JWT and Ogilvy win the business because there is a level of assured success and protection should the worst happen.

I'm not suggesting you do not evaluate those agencies. I'm merely suggesting that their name carries little weight when it comes to making the right decisions. They should be evaluated against the same parameters as the other options. This goes for any type of partner, whether it's a public relations firm or a janitorial service. Here are a few considerations for the next time you embark on finding a partner:

Decide on the details

Before you ask someone for something, you need to know what you need and want. That may sound silly to even read, but you'd be surprised how often companies ask agencies and other partners for services without truly understanding the details. Understanding the details of what you need and want will help the process of identifying partners much easier on you and your team.

Identify decision criteria

How will you know when it's the right fit? What criteria will you and the team use to pinpoint a partner that fits the bill? IF you don't know these things before getting into the search process, stop immediately. You have to know what criteria will be used to evaluate potential partners and how that evaluation will happen. Many companies and leaders will create a ranking system, or rubric, to make the evaluation process more efficient and measurable. I think this is a great move as it removes the "gut" and intuition aspect of the selection process.

Set a budget

One of the biggest time wasters for both agency and potential client is the numerous phone calls and interactions during a pitch or proposal, only to find out that the budget required isn't there. Very few people like to discuss money, but in this world and this scenario, it's best to do yourself and your prospective partners a big favor and make the budget very clear. Why leave it unknown only to find out there isn't enough money to retain services? There is no need to be embarrassed about the budget. It is what it is. Best to make it clear and save everyone time, money, and stress.

Compile an RFP

A Request for Proposal is an important document that outlines the details of the engagement and/or relationship. I'm a firm believer that every project and every relationship should start with one. Not just an overview and some details on what's being asked, but also the details of timing and financials associated with the project. When are responses due? When will they be evaluated? When are you going to make a decision? These all should go into an RFP and be delivered to the partners who are in contention for the work.

Compare apples to apples

In my experience, I have lost opportunities. I know, it's a big shock to me every time, too. But it happens. I am perplexed when I lose an opportunity to an agency that really doesn't align with Vigor—for instance, an agency that's much larger with much more bandwidth and in-house talent—or a smaller 1-2 person studio that calls itself an "agency." Or, at worst, we lose to another company whose capabilities are nothing like ours because the client didn't know what they wanted until they saw it. Please, ensure you're comparing agencies that are similar in size and skill and save everyone the heartache.

Share who's at the table

There are folks who refuse to divulge who else has been asked to provide proposals or participate in a pitch. I can't understand the thinking behind this. Maybe it's a fear of collaborating behind the client's back to align on pricing? However, if you've selected agencies that are similar in size and skill, then pricing should be comparable. For the agency leaders, knowing who else is at the table can help them position their pitches to better suit your needs. Clients win in the end in this scenario because they get tailored information and details unique to their needs as opposed to generalities.

Inform all parties of decisions

You've made the choice and there are going to be some losers. It's part of the game, and no one faults you for it. That is until you decide to go silent and not tell the folks who were not selected. That's, quite honestly, a jerk move. Inform the unselected parties of the decision and be available for a debrief to answer any questions they may have. Agencies pour thousands, if not tens of thousands of dollars into pitches and proposals. I think you can offer 30 minutes to give them some details they can use to grow and get better. Don't you?

These are a few things to consider to help you find talented and strong partners for your brand. It doesn't matter what type of partner you're looking for. The needs are the same. Make sure you have identified your budget for time and financials. Make sure you know how you will evaluate the options. And do inform winners and losers as soon as you can. When you do this, it makes your brand look good even to those who didn't win the chance to collaborate with you.

Onboard partners for success

Every partner that works with the company should have a deep understanding of the brand's strategy and its nuances in order to serve the company effectively. How can a partner do what's right for the brand if they don't know much about it? Only by sheer luck unless someone from the organization invests the time to onboard the group and ensure understanding of the brand is fostered throughout the relationship.

Some companies don't feel like they need to understand the brand. And in some cases that may be true. For instance, the HVAC company probably doesn't have much need for understanding the values and strategic details of a brand in order to complete the job. But what would happen if they did understand the brand a bit deeper? Would they develop a connection to the brand stronger than they had before? Could they turn into proselytizers of the brand and its Purpose? Would there be a downside to investing the time to bring them into the fold?

Successful brands know that brand-building isn't just for the marketers, and it doesn't solely include leadership. Everyone throughout the organization must be stewards of the brand, and everyone that works with the organization should develop stewardship as well. When this happens, brands grow strong and leaders can rest assured that the various teams are working to collectively build the brand better than before.

Public relations firms, architects, advertising agencies, and other companies that focus on different parts of the brand's marketing have a tendency to pay lip service to brand strategies but quickly embark on creating their own paths for the brand. Initial meetings are all hunky-dory with heads nodding and excitement around the brand, but soon after they begin their own research and discovery process replicating tasks that have already been completed.

One time, we were working with a single-unit brand that wanted to scale. That focus was fueled by outside investors who believed in the product the restaurant was putting into the world, but they also realized the name was a problem and, with it, the brand's identity. Vigor was set to task on developing the strategic foundations of the brand's strategy and how it would manifest in a name and identity. Mission accomplished, but we needed to bring in an architecture firm that could absorb the brand strategy and collaborate with both the client and Vigor to develop the full expression of the newly rebranded concept.

I brought to the table an architecture partner I had previously worked with for the client to review and consider. Admittedly I had only worked with this firm once before, and the client had been a nightmare. Despite that particular client's shortcomings, I had thought the interaction with this architecture firm was a good one and that they'd be great collaborators. After all, they certainly talked about this with passion and fervor in our meetings.

After the initial calls and meetings with my client, the architect went silent. About two months later my client asked for a quick check-in with us to review progress. I, of course, was excited to see where the project stood. I was shocked at what was presented to me.

The architecture firm had redesigned the brand's logo and color palettes completely. When I confronted the principal, his response was "well, the client didn't know his 'why' statement, so we felt compelled to fix that." Needless to say, I was fuming. If the client didn't know their why statement, then how was a logo redesign going to help? I expressed this to him and the client and got a flimsy response that didn't address the issue.

That particular client lost its financing halfway through the project, and the project was canceled. However, the damage had been done. I will never refer work to that architecture partner again, period. But where did things go wrong?

First, we should have done a better job at enforcing the importance of the brand strategy and for the leadership to not only hear the purpose and other platforms but fully understand and invest in them. We should have been more pressing with the client to perform due diligence and go through the right process with procuring an architectural partner. Finally, I had to forgive myself for bringing in an uncollaborative group that didn't see Vigor as the strategists and stewards we truly are.

Every partner should be onboarded and fully buy-in to the brand and its strategy. They should not have to dive into brand discovery or moodboarding outside of the nuances required for their specific workstream. They should not introduce anything new to the brand unless it's truly on-brand from top to bottom. It's infuriating when this happens and should be fought tooth and nail by you and other brand representatives.

Brand representatives at the company should take the time necessary to foster brand understanding, evaluate how much the potential partner buys in, and be open to onboarding several times during the relationship. Many companies work with a lot of other clients, so one meeting may not be enough to foster the understanding necessary to create a strong partnership through brand stewardship. Make the time and take the time necessary to build that understanding in every partner, and you'll find yourself with a rockstar team that works well together. And the brand will greatly benefit.

Final Thoughts

Building brands that charge ahead of the herd is no easy business. It takes guts like wrestling down a bucking bull in the Jallikatu games. You have to be a bull in a china shop and challenge the rules and what feels comfortable. You have to be ready to zig when others zag,, even though it feels uncomfortable.

Competition in this world is fierce, and in the restaurant industry it's ruthless and cutthroat. While branding will never make up for a poor business model and finances, it will push a well-operated brand to the forefront. Strong branding can break the mold. It can grab attention, deliver value, and seed memory helping to propel it forward with the core Patrons and those in the sphere of influence.

I encourage you to challenge yourself constantly. To push for innovation just as the Javanese did with their baby bull. You don't have to be a goliath to take down a goliath. A smart "David" will work quite well, as the Biblical parable lays out.

9. Charging Ahead

Brands are made of people, and they are for people. Therefore, human brands are the most attractive. Humans have a purpose, a personality, things they do, and methods for them to present themselves to the world. As do brands. Understanding these details and developing clear insights into what makes your brand unique and wonderful will help you connect with people at levels much deeper than the utility of sating hunger or thirst.

But that's not to discount the important role food plays. You must have consistently delicious food, now more than ever. Half-assed, sort of good food isn't going to cut it. Safe isn't going to cut it. You have to stay clever and always be innovating and thinking of what's next to stay ahead of the herd.

Branding and marketing aren't set-it-and-forget-it endeavors. They require stewardship from the top-down, inside out to continue on the path ahead and never become dated and dusty. With the right leadership, dedicated to the brand's true strategic foundations, any brand can rise from a small multi-unit to a global powerhouse. It takes vision, intelligence, guts, and a bullhearted team to build and scale a bullhearted brand.

It's hard to finish writing a book knowing that there is so much yet to cover and so much left unaddressed. However, my goal was to be informative, helpful, and insightful, with the hopes that this will spark readers to dig deeper and develop a more nuanced knowledge of branding and marketing. I hope I accomplished that goal, and I hope I have set your heart into bull-mode. Charge on!

Further Reading & Listening

By no means is *The Bullhearted Brand* meant to be an end-all, be-all. It scratches the surface on some topics that take years to master. I encourage readers to continue the journey of education and knowledge building through as many resources as possible. To encourage that and point you in the right direction, I've compiled this list of additional books and resources so you can continue the charge.

Note: I suggest purchasing these books through www.bookshop.org. This company gives money back to independent bookstores, which I believe will make the world a better place.

Grits & Grids
A daily collection of branding and design work for the food, beverage, and hospitality space / www.gritsandgrids.com

Forktales Podcast
A bi-weekly podcast with restaurant and hospitality leaders hosted by yours truly, Joseph Szala / www.forktales.co

Start with Why: How Great Leaders Inspire Everyone to Take Action
A pivotal, profound book on brand strategy by Simon Sinek / www.simonsinek.com

What Great Brands Do: The Seven Brand-Building Principles That Separate the Best from the Rest
Denise Lee Yohn dives into the seven principles of great brands and brand building in this book / www.deniseleeyohn.com/brand-book

Fusion: How Integrating Brand and Culture Powers the World's Greatest Companies
Denise Lee Yohn covers the merger of culture and brand strategy with great ideas on activating it in your own brand / www.deniseleeyohn.com/fusion

Onward: How Starbucks Fought for Its Life Without Losing Its Soul
Howard Shultz unfurls his journey and the journey of Starbucks in this profound account that gives a peek behind the curtain.

Archetypes in Branding:
This workbook by Margaret Hartwell is a fantastic resource for a high-level understanding of archetypes. It also includes archetype cards that are invaluable tools for brand strategy / www.archetypesinbranding.com

The Hero and The Outlaw: Building Extraordinary Brands Through the Power of Archetypes
For a deep understanding of archetypes, this book by Margaret Mark and Carol Pearson is second to none.

Contagious: Why Things Catch On
Why does one trend catch on and another die-off? What drives the latest craze? Author Jonah Berger taps psychology and science to identify the principles that make things contagious / jonahberger.com/books/contagious/

Storyscaping: Stop Creating Ads, Start Creating Worlds
A brilliant book by Gaston Legorburu that covers developing brand stories and how they fuel better advertising.

Designing Brand Identity: An Essential Guide for the Whole Branding Team
Alina Wheeler has multiple editions of this text, each one better than the next. It is essential reading and understanding for anyone who creates identities / www.designingbrandidentity.info

Selling Eating: Restaurant Marketing Beyond the Word "Delicious"

Charlie Hopper unpacks how to advertise restaurant brands and their food in a way that's driven by more than hunger and thirst / www.sellingeating.com

Differentiate or Die: Survival in Our Era of Killer Competition

This pivotal book by Jack Trout dives into effective differentiation in order to stay competitive in today's world. Despite being over twenty years old, the thinking and theory still ring true.

Positioning: The Battle for Your Mind

Al Ries and Jack Trout's legendary book on how to position brands for success.

Zag: The Number One Strategy of High-Performance Brands

A small text by Marty Neumeier focused on doing things differently than everyone else and why that works / www.martyneumeier.com/zag

The Brand Gap: How To Bridge The Gap Between Business Strategy and Design

Marty Neumeier connects the dots between strategy and how it manifests visually / www.martyneumeier.com/the-brand-gap

Don't Call It That: A Workbook for Naming Your Product, Business, or Brand

Professional friend, Eli Altman, lays the groundwork and path for successful brand naming / www.extracurricularpress.com/products/dont-call-it-that-second-edition

Index

A Hundred Monkeys, 146
Aesop, 39
Altman, Eli, 146
Alzheimer's, 122
Amazon, 73
America, 177
American Express, 102
amplifiers, 193
Apple, 63, 98
Arby's, 205
Archetypes in Branding, 103
Archetypes, 99-103
Atlanta, Georgia, 89
audience, 58-59, 61-62
Augmented Reality, 171-172
automation, 240-241

Babe the Blue Ox, 249
Banana Republic, 140
Big Mac®, 226
BMW, 31

Boston Consulting Group's Growth-Share Matrix, 157
brand activation, 175
advocacy, 31-32, 195
champion, 57, 176
equity, 225-226
evolution, 223, 234
identity, 25-26, 33, 226
perception, 95, 135
personality, 45, 95, 107-113, 156
representatives, 258
strategy, 36, 226
unity, 41
Brand Standards Book, 154
branding agencies, 24
brand-launch event, 236
brandscape, 144
Brick River Cider Co., 146
Buddhism, 179

Index

budget, 253
bull in a china shop, 22
Bunyan, Paul, 249
Burger King, 78, 232
buyer's remorse, 24

Captain D's, 118
cartoneria, 183
Castro, Fidel, 115
channel, 187
Chen Design, 102
Chicago Bulls, 50
Chick-Fil-A, 170
Chipotle, 32, 66-68
Clif Bar, 102
competition, 27, 71, 75-82
concerned world citizen, 32
Confetti Kitchen, 146
consistency, 154
conversions, 194
CRM systems, 62
Cuban Revolution, 115
cultural alignment, 65
customer relationship management software, 239

Darwin's theory of evolution, 75
Denver, Colorado, 145
destinations, 193
digital marketing analytics, 62
drivers, 193

ecosystem theory, 192
ecosystem, 190, 192
eegee, 241-247
Environmental & Social Governance (ESG), 238
environmentalism, 239
Erik's DeliCafé, 201, 229
Esri's tapestry search, 62
Explorer archetype, 102

Facebook, 31
Farm Burger, 79
"Farm-to" movement, 109
farm-to-table, 30
fast-casual model, 241
Ferdinand, 92
Feria Nacional de la Pirotecnia, 183
Fire It Up: Building Restaurant Brands, 15
Fitch, 245
Five Guys, 78
Five Whys, 104-107
Ford, Henry, 143
Ford Motor Company, 74
forward-thinking design, 63
Fountainhead, 24
franchise system, 230

Gandhi, Mahatma, 114
generalist brand, 59-60

Golden Lasso, 43, 46, 180
Golden State Warriors, 51
Google, 168
Grandma Betty's Biscuit Powder, 74
graphic design, 25
Grindhouse, 79
Grits & Grids, 162
Groupon, 214
Guevara, Che, 114-115

Herfst, Stephen, 59
Hero archetype, 103
Hero & The Outlaw, 102
Hidden Rhythm, 146
Hinduism, 128
Hotel Indigo, 102
Huffington Post, 215
human
    as a lens, 35
    behaviors, 100
    psyche, 64
human resources, 66
Huntsman, Johnny, 121
Hyndman, Sarah, 135

I'm Eddie Cano, 145
inconsistency, 234
India
    independence from British rule, 114
    state of Tamil Nadu, 19
Industrial era, 74
Influence, 60
Innocent archetype, 102
insolvency, 224
Instagram, 17-18, 64, 209

Jackson, Phil, 50
Jacob Faithful, 22
Jallikattu, 19
Javanese, 70
Jewish, 128
John of God, 183
Johnny's Pizza House, 121
Jordan, Michael, 50
Journal of Consumer Research, 135
Judeo-Christian Bible, 128
Jung, Carl, 100

Kangayam, 19
Karate Kid, 75
Kaufman, Alexander, 215
Kerr, Steve, 50
Kia, 31
Komen, Susan G., 122
Krishna, Aradhna, 135

Lee, Bruce, 47
Lexington, Kentucky, 166
LinkedIn, 83
logo, 36, 147-149

London, 22
Longhorn Steakhouse, 203
Louisiana, 121
LuluLemon, 63

Madrid bullfights, 92
magic bullet, 188-189
marketing
    campaign, 200-201
    evergreen, 200-201
Marryat, Frederick, 22
Matrix trilogy, 116
Mattu Pongal day, 19
McDonald's, 78, 226
menu design, 157
merger, 224
Mississippi River, 147, 249
mom-and-pop, 33
momentum, 188
Morpheus, 116
Morrin, Maureen, 135
Moses, 129
multi-unit, 233
Munro Leaf, 93
My Neighbor Felix, 145

National Geographic, 102
NBA, 50
NCAA, 174
negative press, 224
Neumeier, Marty, 85

nirvana, 179
nón lá, 180

Ohno, Taiichi, 104
Old Testament, 128
omnichannel, 240
OrangeTheory, 63
Outlaw archetype, 115
owned channel ecosystem, 65

Pamplona, Spain, 183
Pamplonada, 183
Panera, 141
Patagonia, 102
Patron, 43-44, 195-199
Perceptual Map, 84
pho, 177-178
Phoenix, Arizona, 241
Pippen, Scottie, 50
plant-based, 232
point of sale, 87, 240
Poised, 60
poke bowls, 29
Pokémon Go, 172
Ponce City Market, 173
Positioning, 46, 72-74, 86
Positioning: The Battle for your Mind, 72
Presentation, 45-46, 95, 156
Prius, 63
Product, 45, 95, 116

Project, 44
Projection, 61
Prominence, 60
publicity, 194, 224
Pulikulam, 19
Purpose, 45, 95

QR codes, 173
QSR experience, 66
quick-service, 159, 223

Rand, Ayn, 24
ranking system, 252
rebranding, 222-224, 242
Red Lobster, 118
Request for Proposal, 253
RetailMeNot, 214
Rhames, Ving, 205
Ries, Al, 72
Ritz Carlton, 162
Rize, 89
Roark, Howard, 24
Rodman, Dennis, 52
rule of seven, 187
Ruler archetype, 103
Running of the Bulls, 183
Running with the Bulls, 16

Sage archetype, 102
Saigon, 178-179
service, 119
Shake Shack, 78

Sheppard, Nick, 159
Sinek, Simon, 96
single-unit restaurant, 33
SlapFish, 118-119
slogan, 205
Smashburger, 79
Snapchat, 172
social justice, 239
St. Louis, Missouri, 146
stakeholder, 58-59, 175
Starbucks, 27, 31-32
Steak N' Shake, 78
Sumatra, 70
Sunchasers, 242
sustainability, 67
sustainable, 34
SWOT analysis, 83

table stake, 29
target market, *see* audience
technological integration, 239
TedTalk, 96
TGI Friday's, 158, 215-217
Tin Cup Whiskey, 102
Tipping Point, 191
"tribe" culture, 141
touchpoints, 131, 146
Toyoda, Sakichi, 104
Toyota Motor Corporation, 104
Trout, Jack, 72
Tucson, Arizona, 241

Tultepec, Mexico, 183
typography, 36, 151

umbrella company, 33

Venn diagram, 42
Vietnam, 177-179
Vietvana, 173, 179-180
Vigor, 14
virtual food halls, 87
Virtual Reality, 171, 174
visual identity, 148-156
visual language, *see* visual identity

Washingtonian, 145
Wayfair, 73
Wendy's, 78
Wheeler, Alina, 96
whitespace, 80, 84
Whole Foods, 63
Wikipedia, 83, 128
Wonder Woman, 43
Wow Bao, 123

Yoda, 116
YumBunz, 124-126

"Zag" strategy, 85
Zaxby's, 169-170, 174